Not
my
fault

I dedicate this book to my husband Craig and four children, they gave me the strength to continue.

Not my fault

TRISH HINDE

With *SUNDAY TIMES BESTSELLING* AUTHOR ANN CUSACK

MIRROR BOOKS

MIRROR BOOKS

All of the events in this story are true, but some
names and details have been changed to protect the
identities of individuals.

© Trish Hinde

1

Published in Great Britain and Ireland in 2024 by
Mirror Books, a Reach PLC business.

www.mirrorbooks.co.uk
@TheMirrorBooks

Print ISBN 9781915306616
eBook ISBN 9781915306623

Printed and bound in Great Britain by
CPI Group (UK) Ltd, Croydon, CR0 4YY

MIX
Paper | Supporting
responsible forestry
FSC® C171272

Contents

Prologue

Flattened against the wall of the landing, I was too frightened to even breathe. I wondered if, like a butterfly, I might camouflage against the wallpaper, in my blue and pink Care Bear pyjamas, and somehow go unnoticed.

Slowly and stealthily, I inched across the dark grey carpet, and with each step, my heart hammered that little bit harder. Dad's bedroom door, always open, was at the top of the stairs and I had to pass it. Was there any other way? The possibilities ricocheted wildly around my head. I imagined myself levitating and floating down the stairs. Or slithering underneath the carpet like a snake. Could I open a window and shimmy down a drainpipe? No.

I crept a little further, holding my breath, and a voice snapped the silence:

"Come in, Tricia."

I had always known it would come. I had always known there was no escape. And yet the shock ripped through me, turning me inside out, and I felt myself collapsing. Like a butterfly, I could have escaped. I could also be crushed.

"Come in," repeated the voice.

I did not dare make him say it a third time. The double bed was in the middle of the room and lying back on the pillows, resplendent in his wickedness, was my father, Gerard King. He was completely naked. His moustache drooped mournfully down either side of his mouth, like a frown. His eyes were sunken, glassy and hard as stones. He patted the bed and, like a lamb to the slaughter, I climbed under the duvet.

During the really bad part, I focussed on the pink and white floral border which ran around the walls of the bedroom. In my mind, I traced the flowery shapes and coloured them in. There was a window to my right, looking out over the street. It struck me as bizarre that there were people passing our house, walking to work, nipping to the shops, glancing up maybe at the bedroom window. Surely there was some sign, some outward betrayal, of the horrors within?

Always, Dad left the door brazenly ajar whilst it was happening. My older siblings were downstairs. But my father, supremely arrogant, knew he was beyond challenge. For a moment, my gaze snagged on the doorway, and there she was, a shimmering, almost transparent woman, with a kind face and a long, full dress.

"Help me," I pleaded silently. "Help me, please."

But in the next moment, she was gone. Spirited away. Even the ghosts in this house were too frightened to speak out. I had nobody on my side, living or dead. So what chance did I have? When Dad was finished with me, he said:

"You know I'm scared of prison. So don't tell anyone. It's not my fault Tricia, it's just the way I am."

Prologue

With the solemnity of a six-year-old, I nodded, staring still at the pink and white border. Dad was asleep within moments, his face to my back, his arm clamped proprietorially across my chest. I lay trapped in the bed, with the arm becoming heavier and heavier, until it felt like a leaden weight, crushing my ribcage. I was small and slight for my age and Dad was overweight and over-bearing.

Carefully, I flattened myself into the mattress and began to ease out from underneath the arm. I slowly wriggled free, almost paralysed by the dread of waking him and the knowledge that, in his fury, he would make me do it all over again. I tip-toed past Dad's work shirt, hanging on the curtain rail from last night's shift. There was a faint whiff of stale sweat and cheap aftershave, and I gagged a little.

Out on the landing, I scurried like a frightened field mouse down the stairs, the blood thumping in my ears, the panic and relief washing through me in equal measure. I could hear Dad's contented snores floating down the stairs. A man sleeping soundly without a thing on his conscience.

In the kitchen, I poured my cereal and watched, moon-eyed, as the cornflakes went soggy and turned to mush. My older brothers and sisters bustled and bickered around me; nobody even noticed I was there. Ours was a shouty, fractured household. We were brought up not to look out for, but to lash out at each other. I slipped out of the front door, and off to school, melting into the morning drizzle in my mismatched uniform, with Dad's snores and pitiful lies ringing in my ears.

'It's not my fault. It's just the way I am.'

1

Hide Away

WILMSLOW, CHESHIRE. SPRING 1993

"If you miss your jump, you land in the sludge," said my friend, Lisa, in a matter-of-fact voice. Her blue eyes narrowed as she surveyed the steps and her vivid red hair swung from side to side in a ponytail. I balanced on the top step, preparing my launch, trying not to think about the sludge.

"And if you land in the sludge, the crocodiles will eat you," she added cheerfully, as I bent my knees.

Holding my breath, I closed my eyes and banished all thoughts of crocodiles as I propelled myself through the air. It felt like such a long way, as my five-year-old legs paddled furiously and seemed to pause mid-flight. Landing clumsily on the steps at the other side, I grazed my knee, but the sense of victory, and the dizzying relief of survival, was enough to dull the pain.

"You did it!" Lisa yelled triumphantly, clapping her hands together. "No dinner for the crocodiles today. Hurray for you, Trish."

Before she could take her turn braving the crocodile sludge, Lisa's mum came to call her in for tea and I, reluctantly, walked the two streets back to my own house where I lived with my parents, Gerard and Joan, and my five older siblings. Wilmslow, Cheshire, was an upmarket town, home to lots of celebrities and footballers. There were Coronation Street stars rubbing shoulders with Manchester United players; Porsches, Lamborghinis and Ferraris parked on the high street. But we lived on the town's only council estate, a world away from the luxury and the glamour. A world away, it seemed to me, from true happiness.

In our four-bedroom house, there were eight people, two dogs, two Guinea pigs, three rabbits and two hamsters. The guinea pigs, Snowy and Toffee, lived in a tank in my bedroom, the rabbits, Floppy, Thumper and Popsy, and hamsters, Po and Lala, were in the shed. In addition, my paternal granddad and uncle, who lived nearby, were often at the house too. It was chaotic, cramped and, above all, it was angry.

"Where do you think you've been?" my father demanded as I sidled up to the dining table and silently took my place. "You get in here on time or you don't get fed. Understand?"

I stared down at my sausage and oven chips, thankful for the sniping and squabbling around me, because Dad soon transferred his attention onto my older siblings, and I was left to pick at my meal in peace.

"You lot can clear this mess away," Dad announced, as he mopped his plate with a slice of white bread and lumbered into the living room to watch television.

We had lists of chores pasted on the wall in the kitchen and it was my job to clean the bathroom and the toilet and empty the bins. But I didn't dare object to this extra task and, grabbing a tea towel, I helped dry the dishes whilst one of my sisters washed. It could, should, have been fun. I was the youngest in the family; we could have thrown soap suds and played daring games of catch with the dishes and plates. But there was no camaraderie, no friendship between us. The atmosphere was frosty and resentful, as if merely being in the same room with each other was a chore in itself.

"Make sure you dry the cutlery properly," reminded one of my brothers sharply. "Or we'll all get a smack round the head."

We couldn't bite back against our father. And so, we turned our pent-up frustrations on each other. Dad's voice suddenly boomed across the kitchen like a thunderclap.

"Someone get in here and find the remote NOW," he bawled, and my brothers stiffened as though they had been electrocuted, before hurrying into the living room to find the missing TV remote control.

I knew I didn't have the remote, but I checked my pockets automatically, neurotically. I was always on edge. This constant, gnawing unease was at the core of our family. Many families had a loving mum or a hard-working dad at their centre. Some were lucky enough to have both. But we had a nucleus of pure fear. Right from being a toddler, I had learned to be wary of my father. He was a big man; thick set and heavy, with an exaggerated handle-bar moustache. On another dad, it might have been quirky, comical perhaps, but there was nothing remotely funny about my father.

He was especially cruel to our Staffordshire Bull Terriers, Tyson and Bonnie. Sometimes, he'd come home from work in a bad mood and boot the dogs, as he would a football, simply because he could. Simply because they were there. Cowering behind a chair, or hidden under the table, I winced in silent, impotent, revulsion, as Dad waded in, kicking and swearing at the poor animals, blaming them for his bad day at work or his disappointing family.

"And stop howling, you useless bloody mutt!" he yelled. "Or I'll shut you up for good!"

Part of me felt heartbroken for my pets and their pain. But another part of me quivered with the knowledge that I was surely next in line. I clung to the legs of the dining chair and screwed my eyes tightly shut, hoping I might make myself invisible, hoping I might somehow evaporate into the ether, so Dad would forget all about me. But sometimes, even with my eyes closed, in my hiding place, I could sense my father's anger brewing, like a far-off storm.

I used to think I could feel his temper rising before he even knew it himself, almost as though I was a type of mood barometer. As a little girl, I could forecast a change in tone the same way in which some people could predict a rain shower. It was not any kind of gift or foresight. I think it was more of an instinct, sharpened and honed by necessity and a practical sense of self-preservation. I'd watch, mesmerised and terrified, as Dad's pupils grew larger, and his eyes, always sunken, seemed to dip further into the crevasses of his face. It was coming, I knew it. Then, the final straw, he would stub out his cigarette in his big glass ashtray; a sure sign he was about to let rip.

When his fury finally burst through the surface, it was as if a bomb was detonating, and I scampered, like my pet hamster, across the kitchen and up the stairs to the temporary and illusory safety of my shared bedroom. I grabbed my teddy-bear, Gizmo, and told him:

"Don't worry, he won't come up here."

Gizmo had rubber ears and slept on the pillow with me, each night. He stared back at me, impassively, as the shouting continued. My words of reassurance were more for me than him. But even then, in the bedroom, there was no true respite. I had to share dilapidated and collapsing red bunk beds with an older sibling. I was on the bottom bunk, and I lived in mortal fear of the top bunk breaking a little bit more and the red metal crushing me in my sleep.

There was no real hiding place in my home. No safe haven.

Someone, presumably my father, had removed all the inside door handles, so once the doors were shut, there was no way out, or no easy way at least. We kept an old butter knife under the bed to do the job. Late at night, when the sound of shouting downstairs was keeping me awake, I'd turn the butter knife quietly inside the door and then crouch on the prickly carpet at the door of the bedroom, listening to the arguing, and with my nightie pulled right over my knees to keep warm.

The argument was just background noise, as much an accepted part of life as the sound of traffic or barking dogs. As the row inevitably grew physical, I covered my ears to blot out the sound of smashing glass or slamming doors, and I hugged my knees tighter to me still. My main worry was for Tyson and Bonnie, who might be caught in the crossfire. They slept on the living room sofas and so often were in the thick of it all.

"Hide away," I whispered, hoping I might reach them psychically. "Get into the garden. Or the shed. Just hide."

It was a relief each morning to run downstairs and find the dogs alive and unharmed and waiting for me to take them out to play. And so, the best part of my home life was actually not at home at all. I had most of my fun either with my dogs outside, or visiting my friend Lisa, who was two streets away, but felt so much closer. She and I were the same age and had the same sense of mischief and bright imagination.

In the local square, there were two grassy platforms, linked by two sets of steps, and Lisa and I played for hours, jumping from one set of steps to the other, desperately trying to avoid the small patch of concrete in the middle, where the mythical man-eating crocodiles lived. Little did I know, as I screeched and squealed in horrified delight, that the real danger was lurking right in the heart of my own home.

2

A Typical Family

Born prematurely, at 28 weeks, and weighing only 1.5kg, I spent most of my early childhood in and out of Macclesfield District General Hospital in Cheshire. I was a winter baby, born on Bonfire Night 1987, and according to my parents, I was often sickly and unwell. I was asthmatic and picked up chest infections, viral wheezes and stomach bugs, one after the other.

I spent two, three days at most in hospital on each occasion, until I was fit enough to be discharged, and I don't remember missing home at all during those times. My parents didn't usually visit whilst I was in hospital; my father said there were no suitable buses or no suitable times. We did have a family car but, with three jobs between him and my mother, and five other siblings to consider, the car was usually in demand.

"You'll be alright on your own, won't you, Tricia?" said my father, and I understood it was more of a statement than a question.

Well, I would have to be. But again, I quite enjoyed the break from the commotion and chaos at home. There was something so lovely and comforting about lying between clean, crisp sheets, with my eyes closed, listening to the soothing background hum of the ward staff, the trolleys as they trundled past, the distant town centre traffic.

The nurses made such a fuss of me and even the families of the other patients stopped to smile and ask how I was; a child in hospital without a visitor is rare, and, starved of the right kind of attention at home, I lapped it up and I loved it. The nurses brought me chocolate biscuits and extra helpings of pudding too.

"You need to put some meat on those bones," they told me. "You're far too thin."

I was often weak and lacking calories when I went into hospital, but always eating well and starting to gain weight by the time I left. Once when I was on the children's ward, a nurse ran me a lovely bubble bath and washed my long blonde hair. She had such a kind face and was so gentle, washing and rinsing my hair over and over, letting me luxuriate in the warm bubbles like a pint-sized princess.

"You're going to smell beautiful by the time I've finished with you," the nurse beamed.

Afterwards, she brushed my hair and blow dried it and made me a hot chocolate in the ward kitchen, before tucking me back up in my bed.

"You've never been so squeaky clean!" she announced.

I felt as though I was floating on my own little cloud of happiness, and I packaged away that golden memory of the hospital bath time as one of the most enjoyable events of my entire childhood. It was only as an adult, I remembered with dismay that I was usually under siege from a plague of head lice when I was admitted to hospital. The nurse was probably washing and re-washing my hair to get rid of all the bugs! The realisation took some of the polish off my shiny memory, but the lustre could not be dulled completely.

As a child, being in hospital was the nearest thing I got to having a little holiday, and there was always a tinge of regret when it came time for me to go home again. Besides, my parents were short of money and often in debt, and we couldn't afford real holidays.

Mum worked two jobs, as a carer overnight and in a plastics factory during the day. She had various jobs in fast food places and in various retail outlets too. Dad worked shifts as a security guard and later, as a long-distance lorry driver. He was out either overnight or until late at night, and so was the main carer for the younger children in the house. Mum was hardly ever at home during the day.

With six children, Dad liked to remind us there was no money for holidays or days out. Despite this, my father was a heavy smoker, and he had a TV sports package so he could watch all of his beloved Manchester United matches. Looking back now, it seems as though our poverty was prioritised in a way that it hit him the least, if at all. Yet if that was the case, those little bonuses didn't make him any more pleasant to be around.

Dad seemed to wake up in a bad temper and it got progressively worse during the day. When he wasn't at work, or in bed, he'd lie on the sofa, watching TV, with the sound turned up loud. I'd hear him calling me, down from my bedroom, or even in from the garden, and into the living room, to carry out his demands.

"Close that blind," he ordered, from his prone position on the sofa; a large, beached walrus with his ridiculous moustache. "The sun's in my eyes."

Inwardly, I cursed him for being lazy and selfish; making me run from the other end of the house like a hired help when he was lying right next to the blind himself. I would never have dared say it out loud, but he must have read my mind, or perhaps he was just slap happy, because as I walked past the sofa, he flicked out a hand, quick as a lizard's tongue, and whacked me hard on the back of my bare legs.

"You behave yourself," he rapped, even though I had done nothing wrong. Although, as a little girl, I told myself he wouldn't hit me for no reason and so I must have deserved it.

Dad administered most of his punishments whilst lying down on the sofa. It was as though I didn't even merit him sitting upright and taking the matter more seriously. Nothing, not even disciplining his children, could get in the way of him watching Man United or his old Chubby Brown videos.

Another day, I was sitting at the dining table with one of my friends from the estate, who unusually had been allowed to come round to play. I was in a good mood and when Dad came in I felt a sudden and completely misplaced burst of mischief.

"Hello, Ged," I grinned, with the overconfidence of a

young child who has no idea of the trouble they are tumbling into.

Dad spun around clumsily, and I felt the mood change even before he had completed the turn. I could actually hear his temper revving internally, spluttering like an angry engine.

"You show me some respect," he spat, jabbing a nicotine-stained finger in my face. "I'm Dad to you, not Ged, and don't you ever forget it! You're a cheeky little shit!"

For good measure he slapped me on the side of the head.

"That'll teach you," he bawled, causing my poor friend to shrink back in alarm.

But of course it didn't teach me, not at all. I was a little girl; I got into scrapes, and I misbehaved, just like all kids. I couldn't help it. But I was always, always, wary of my father. Like one of my own pet rabbits, poking my nose above ground, I'd sniff the air with caution, searching for signs of his forthcoming fury.

I was not usually allowed to invite friends to the house, and probably they would not have wanted to come, after hearing tales about Dad's temper after the incident in the kitchen. But one afternoon, again with a naïve sense of childish optimism, I asked three friends from my class, who lived on our estate, if they wanted to come over and see my Guinea pigs.

"You just knock on the door, and I'll let you in," I told them.

Somehow, I thought I could sneak them past my dad, and then up the stairs, without being noticed. I just hadn't thought it through. Late in the afternoon, the three girls arrived on the doorstep, and I ran to answer the bell. But as they were standing in the hallway, giggling, Dad yelled:

"You send them home! I'm not having your friends in this house!"

The laughter stopped instantly as if their voice boxes had been cauterised. The three girls turned and ran from the house, and I was mortified. I slunk upstairs, my cheeks burning with shame. I had few enough friends as it was, and now I had lost three more. I dreaded the thought of going into school the next day, facing the inevitable teasing about my father.

"Serves you right!" Dad shouted. "No wonder you've no friends. Nobody likes you anyway. That was all your own fault, Tricia. All your fault."

Dad's temper, whilst it terrified me, did not go beyond the odd punch or whack. I was not beaten to the extent that I had frequent bruises or injuries. I was always in trouble, but then, most kids are. And so, in that respect, our house was not so different to thousands of others.

Dad was a bully; he was cruel and domineering and selfish, and he chipped away at my self-confidence and my childish optimism, like rain eroding a coastline. If it continued, I would simply topple and fall into the sea in broken chunks. He was not a good father. But he was all I knew. And, as a typical kid, I didn't dwell on the negatives.

I had a baseless belief, like most children, that things would always get better. I didn't look past tomorrow, or even past today. Besides, no childhood is truly without enjoyment or pleasure, and there were many advantages to having a mother who was never home and a father who lay on the sofa most days. There was a field at the back of our home, which later became a busy bypass, but we made the most of the space for big games of rounders, involving maybe half the kids on the estate. If Dad was in a good mood, or perhaps he'd had a couple of beers, he'd wander outside to join in. The other parents from the street got involved, rolling up their jeans and running barefoot through the grass, and there was a wonderful, warm feeling of community oozing through us all.

"Come on Trish, your turn to bowl!" shouted Lisa's mum. "You get the next one out and it's ice creams all round, on me."

I giggled with delight as I sent the ball soaring through the air, miles wide of the target, but Lisa's mum bought the ice-creams anyway. I loved those evenings, and in some ways, I felt bonded far more to my neighbourhood than I did to my own family. There was a path from the field through to Bluebell Woods, a woodland area which led down to the railway track.

Me and my friends loved searching out woodland ponds and looking for newts and little fishes. We cradled them like precious jewels in jam jars all the way home until an attack of conscience made me retrace my careful steps back to the pond and throw them into the water.

"There you go little fish, back with your mummy and daddy," I said softly.

As a young girl, I did not see the allegorical message. But it was tragic that I desperately wanted a safe and loving family environment for the fish, whilst I did not have one myself. Yet, on the outside, the familial cracks were pretty well pasted over. At the end of each summer, there was an annual trip to see Blackpool Illuminations, with as many of us crammed into the car as would fit. I remember being dazzled by the light-up toys being sold at the roadside, which my parents, like many others, refused to buy.

"Waste of money," my mother said, which was doubtless what every mother in every car was telling her disappointed children.

Again, outwardly, we were in some respects very typical. Because my birthday was November 5, we usually had a few fireworks in the back garden. I didn't always have a birthday cake, and I never had a party or even a friend round for a birthday tea. But there was enough of a fuss to make me feel happy.

"You going to try to be a good girl this year, Tricia?" my father would ask, on every birthday.

And there it was; a shard of guilt injected into every small sliver of happiness; a weary recognition on my part that I simply had to do better. I was not a naughty or a difficult child; I did as I was told, and I barely even spoke in the house. Yet the sly comments from my dad made me believe I was a problem and a burden.

Each Christmas, me and my siblings got at least one gift each. On Christmas mornings, we were made to eat breakfast together at the dining table before we could open a single present. It sounds a rather formal arrangement, and we were in no way a formal family, but I think now it was more about control and discipline; my father liked to be the one to decide exactly when and where the festivities should begin.

I remember the excitement tingling in my fingers and toes as I peered round the archway which connected our dining and living rooms. From my chair, I could see the artificial Christmas tree, with a small pile of wrapped gifts underneath.

"Can't wait," I whispered to myself, spooning in rice crispies as quickly as I could. "Can't wait."

On Saturday mornings, Dad was in charge, and he would occasionally take us younger ones to the local leisure centre to swim. Though he was overweight and out of shape, he was a strong man and had been a good swimmer when he was younger. He helped out also on the school swim team, coaching the better swimmers and attending galas and competitions. One particular Saturday, I was just about managing to tread water, with my armbands on, when one of my older brothers said:

"Give me those armbands Tricia, I'm going down to the deep end."

Ignoring my feeble protests, he pulled my inflatable bands off each arm and paddled off to the other end of the pool. My head dipped below the water and in panic I gulped in a full chlorinated mouthful. Scrabbling wildly, I sank only further, my arms and legs flailing uselessly as my eyes, wide open, stared upwards through the water. And in an instant, Dad was there. My lifesaver. He yanked me up, from the bottom of the pool, and slapped my back hard. I vomited a milky mixture of water, mucus and tears.

"Give me those armbands!" Dad bellowed across the water, and my brother powered back, from the other side of the pool, in shocked obedience. Dad plonked me on the side of the pool and threw me the armbands, before swimming off himself. It was all very matter of fact and emotionless.

Later it struck me as quite bizarre how Dad made such a fuss about minor events, such as the TV being at the right volume. Yet when something truly momentous did actually happen, and I almost drowned, he barely acknowledged it. For my part, I was troubled by a fear of water from that day at the pool and even now, as an adult, I hate having my face splashed.

Occasionally, perhaps in the school holidays, Dad took us for days out. We went to the zoo once. We sometimes went to the park. Dad came home one warm summer's evening with two kittens, one white with black markings and one black with white socks. They both had adorable pink little noses and big liquid eyes and I fell in love with them. They followed me all round the house and I even sneaked them upstairs to my bedroom, at night. I could fit one in each of my dressing gown pockets. But a couple of days later, as I was calling their names, I discovered the kittens were nowhere to be found. Dad ordered us all to search the house thoroughly, whilst he watched, but we couldn't find the missing animals. I could feel Dad's temper bubbling like a broth.

"Somebody's nicked those kittens," he fumed. "And I'm going to find out who."

He stormed out of the house on the warpath and began hammering on our neighbours' doors. Soon after, he came home carrying a tiny kitten with similar markings to one of ours.

"Found one," he said gruffly. "That family on the corner had it. They didn't admit they'd nicked it, the cheeky buggers. God knows where the other one went."

The kitten didn't look quite the same to me, but I was too wary of my father to say anything. Then a few moments later, both of our kittens came tumbling out of the vent which was attached to the tumble dryer. They had probably been hiding in there, fast asleep, all along.

"Will you take the spare kitten back to its home now, Dad?" I asked timidly.

"No!" he bawled. "And shut up about it! What's it got to do with you?"

I knew better than to push the point. And though I was pleased to have three kittens to play with, deep down I knew it was wrong. Dad had swiped someone else's pet and I rec-ognised how upset I'd be if it happened to me. My heart ached when I thought of the children the kitten had once belonged to, but I was too frightened to take it back.

Over the following months, all three kittens disappeared, one by one, no doubt migrating, as cats often do, to a household offering better food. But I couldn't help feeling it was retribution; I feared I'd been found out, for keeping quiet about the stolen kitten. It was all my fault; everything was my fault. And now, as punishment, I had lost all three.

Another day, I was on the bus with Dad and one of my brothers, going for my asthma check-up at the hospital. I'd had asthma since I was a baby, but it didn't bother me quite as much as Dad always seemed to think. Whilst I stared, absent-mindedly, out of the window, Dad had been chatting, quite pleasantly, with the man in the seat in front. Then without warning he suddenly grabbed the man's hair, pulled it sharply back, and punched him hard in the face.

The violence, close up and raw, took my breath away. But Dad didn't speak. He didn't even seem slightly concerned when blood spurted from the man's nose and the other passengers stared in open-mouthed disbelief. Nobody challenged Dad. They probably had more sense. He simply got up at the next stop, and my brother and I followed, like worried little lemmings. It was yet another example of how quickly Dad's mood could switch. His temper was always lurking, like a burglar in a wardrobe, waiting to pounce.

Occasionally, though she was hardly home, Mum and I baked cheese pie and jam tarts together. I enjoyed carving a 'T' for Tricia, into the pastry and watching my creation browning nicely in the oven. One day, I was helping her to heat up spaghetti hoops for tea. By now, I was learning to read at primary school, and I was like a sponge, eager to soak up as much knowledge as I could. We had precious few books at home and I was keen to read everything I came across. Curiously, I turned the spaghetti tin on its side so I could sound out the ingredients and cooking instructions.

"H-e-a-t in a s-a-u-c-e p-a-n" I said, slowly.

In the next minute, I felt a cold slop onto my dress and my legs.

"Tricia!" Dad bawled. "You've spilled the spaghetti everywhere, you silly little cow! You make a mess of everything.

You're useless. No wonder nobody likes you. You're absolutely thick as shit."

I got a smack across the back of my legs for my stupidity. Worse, I saw Dad aim a crafty kick at Tyson too and that hurt me even more. I had noticed that was another strange quirk of his temper. Often, he was happy to completely explode in public and seemed content to lay into strangers, neighbours and family members alike. Other times, he was secretive and sly with his violence.

From my hiding place, under the table, I caught Dad more than once checking the coast was clear before he grabbed the dog lead and lashed poor Tyson with it, for no reason at all. The poor dog leapt up and howled in pain, but Dad just kept on whipping him with the lead, unaware I was watching. Nobody would ever have dared confront or criticise Dad, so I don't know why he hit the dog in secret. Perhaps he got a special sort of kick out of thinking he was getting away with it.

And so, it was rare for me to spend any time – and even rarer any enjoyable time – with my father. Communication was one-way only, and it was usually fractious and aggressive. Dad spent his time shouting at me. I spent my time trying to go unnoticed. And the occasions of family unity, when they came; the days out, the afternoons spent cooking or playing rounders, fell depressingly short of what they could and should have been. Any kind of closeness between us felt artificial and strained, as though we might, as a household, combust at any moment. Even at the age of six, it already felt too late for us to be a proper family.

3

One of the Kings

With both of my parents out working so much, and a painful lack of affection or care from my father, I quickly became self-sufficient. Even though I had five older siblings, there was no familial bond, no sense of kinship, between us at all. I was really no closer to them than I was to my father. As with my allocated household chores, I didn't look up to them to help me fasten my school shoes or brush my long hair into a ponytail, and neither did they step in to offer.

Mum had taken me for my first day at primary school, in September 1992, but after that, I was on my own. She was usually at work when I was getting up, and Dad was still in bed, following a night shift. With nobody looking over my shoulder, I was happy to skip the inconveniences of showering and brushing my teeth.

I soon learned to get myself up and dressed, quite often wearing a mismatched uniform. The regular school uniform was a grey skirt with a red jumper. But I never seemed to be able to find that combination in the piles of washing which teetered on the arms of chairs and on the edge of the dining table, threatening to topple at any moment. The best I could cobble together was a navy-blue skirt and a bobbly grey cardigan and yesterday's socks turned inside out to hide the stains. I had no pumps, no PE kit, no hat and gloves for winter, no sun-tan lotion in the summer. My teachers never mentioned my hotch-potch outfits, which reassured me that perhaps they hadn't noticed.

Looking back now, I can see they probably felt sorry for me, realised how painfully shy I was, and didn't want to make me feel even worse. For breakfast, I stuck to cereal, unsure yet of how to work the toaster and also unable to reach it, right across the work surface, without pulling up a chair. I didn't have time for that sort of thing.

Each morning, I poured out my rice crispies and listened, with satisfaction, to them popping. It was all part of my routine, and I relied on those pops. They were small signposts, confirming I was successfully making it through my morning tasks.

"Pop, pop, pop," I said to Tyson, as he waited hopefully for scraps at my feet.

After finishing my breakfast, I was always careful to wash my bowl and spoon and put the milk back in the fridge. It was vital not to leave a mess behind if I wanted to stay under the radar and out of trouble with my father. The kitchen was noisy and busy; I was usually jostling for space with older brothers and sisters. Sometimes there wasn't even a spare chair for me, and I ate my breakfast perched on the bottom stair, with Tyson lying on my feet.

The house was jam packed. But I was most definitely alone. I was most definitely lonely. There was no conversation, less still pleasantries, between us all. There was shouting, bickering; the odd time there might be a bit of a scuffle. But that was as far as it went.

Saddest of all to me now, is that when my chores were done, I pulled on my coat and shoes and slipped out of the house unceremoniously. There was nobody to see me off, to kiss me goodbye, to hand me a packed lunch or a freshly laundered PE kit. I blended into the morning air, little more than a willo' the wisp, a trick of the light, a forgotten child.

When I look back on my six-year-old self, my heart bleeds at her morning school routine. I want to rewind, take her face in my hands, and tell her how much she is cherished. I wish I could make sure she had her woolly gloves and hat, or her sunscreen and a bottle of water. I wish someone was there, looking out for her.

But the cold fact is, I had nobody.

It was just a 10-minute walk to school, and often I'd catch up with classmates and their parents, following the same route. I was timid and withdrawn and didn't speak unless someone spoke to me first. There were some families who purposely avoided me too.

"Oh, she's one of the Kings," they said, exchanging a knowing look, and that was the only explanation they needed.

Our family was notorious on the estate because we were rough and poor. I know now, from medical notes, our home was unhygienic; I often had head lice and my clothes were dirty. But back then, of course, I had nothing to compare it to. It wasn't until after I started school, I realised it wasn't normal to have head lice. The schoolyard was ruthlessly cruel and as soon as their parents were out of earshot some of the kids turned on me.

'Don't play with her! She's got lice! She's infected!'

'Ugh, she's making me itchy just looking at her!'

And in class:

'Miss, I can't sit next to Tricia King. I'm worried about catching her nits. Is it true they burrow into your brain? Is that why she's not very clever?'

It was merciless. There was one other girl who, like me, was usually battling an infestation and she and I would check each other's hair like little primates and pull out the lice, one by one.

Our routine, designed to make us more socially accept- able, ironically alienated our classmates even further, and I had even fewer friends at school. The teachers made excep- tions for me, I'd get away with the wrong colour school jumper or losing my reading book or arriving late. It wasn't unusual either for me to fall asleep with my head on my desk, because I was so tired, and the teachers simply let me rest. But that was as far as it went. Nobody stepped in with specific concerns, or if they did, I never got to know about them. I was never offered practical help or questioned about my background and my home life.

For my part, I worked hard to remain as unobtrusive as possible. I was a people pleaser; obedient, passive and compliant, as closed-in and impenetrable as a stone statue. As at home, I simply wanted to paddle through each day, unnoticed. I felt as though I was swimming just above the surface, almost out of sight, but also in danger of gulping in a mouthful of water and choking. I was treading water and treading a fine line. I was coping, I was bobbing at the edge. But only just.

Though Lisa and I attended different primary schools, she and I played together after school was finished. And her mother, unlike most others, welcomed me with open arms. Whilst we played on the steps, she'd often walk down to the square, carrying two brews and a plate of rich tea fingers.

"My favourites," I beamed.

"I know they are," she replied, and her eyes twinkled.

I was often invited to stay for tea with Lisa and if it wasn't a school night, we'd maybe have a sleepover. She had bunk beds, like me, but hers were not on the verge of collapse and I always slept far more peacefully in her bedroom than I did in my own. Lisa was an only child and her parents had bought bunk beds especially for sleepovers. Especially for me, I liked to think. As we lay in bed, her in the top bunk, me in the bottom, we sang songs and planned out new dance routines.

"What about me doing a backwards roll at the end whilst you sing the chorus again?" I suggested. "Can I borrow your sparkly hairband? You've got loads."

"Course you can," Lisa replied. "Let's do the dance tomorrow."

The next morning, Lisa's mum had bacon butties and hot

chocolates waiting for us. And afterwards, she pushed the kitchen table ceremonially to one side, in preparation for the big show. She oohed and aahed and clapped and whooped in all the right places, as we performed our latest routine.

"Wow, you girls really should be on the telly," she told us, with a perfectly straight face. "You have so much talent."

I loved those days at Lisa's. They were just an ordinary family, but that was exactly what I craved. Lisa had a stay-at-home mum and her dad worked as a builder. Her mum was everything I wanted in a parent; affectionate, gentle, reliable. I appreciated her generosity more than she would ever know. But there is always a flip side to such happiness, and feeling her warmth made going home to my father feel so much colder and lonelier.

"You can come and stay again next weekend," Lisa told me. "We can do a new dance next time. Backflips maybe. You can borrow my leotard with the sequins on. Promise."

That night, in my own bedroom, I stared at the net curtains at the windows which had yellowed with age and smoke and had a crusty brown rim around the edges. I felt a jolt of anxiety at the thought of the door without a handle; I was stuck in here; cornered.

Hour after hour, I lay in my rickety bunk bed, watching the mattress above sagging, and the red metalwork straining. I worried it would all, one day, come crashing down upon me.

4

The Ghost Lady

One morning, in the autumn of 1993, I woke as usual for school with the sound of angry voices stabbing through my sleepiness. The routine kitchen debacle had begun. It was chilly, with a nip of early frost in the air outside, and I was glad of my fleecy Care Bear pyjamas as I jumped out of bed and padded quietly across the landing. Reaching my parents' bedroom door, which was ajar, I heard my dad's voice, saying:

"Tricia? In here. Come on."

I never disobeyed him. But this time, for some reason, I stopped, like a small animal, sensing a predator. My skin prickled and my whole body was alert. Even out on the landing, I could almost sense his nostrils quivering. I imagined his dark, bottomless, eyes becoming blacker still. I heard him clear his throat, like a growl, and I hurried into his room and stood at the doorway.

Dad patted the space on the double bed beside him. When I did not move, he flung back the duvet and said: "Here."

Desperately, as I walked towards the bed, I tried to tell myself this was not necessarily a bad thing. My older siblings were downstairs. I could even hear people passing underneath the window. Yet the impression of foreboding was so strong it almost choked me; it had me by the throat. I didn't know what was coming but I knew I was very afraid.

Once I was in the bed, Dad quickly pulled down my blue and pink pyjama bottoms. I lay rigid and terrified, my six-year-old self completely unaware of what was happening but at the same time weighed down with a terrible knowledge that this was a line gouged in the sand. After this, there was no going back. I yelped out involuntarily, in discomfort, and Dad hissed:

"Quiet, Tricia. You must be quiet. And don't tell anyone. You mustn't tell a soul."

And yet the bedroom door was open, with several, maybe all, of my older siblings downstairs. Could this be such a bad thing if he was happy to keep the bedroom door open? I remembered his habit of secretly hitting Tyson when he felt nobody was watching. Did he get a kick out of abusing me, with people nearby, as he did when he hurt the dog, somehow baiting discovery? I was perplexed. Yet how could this be right when I was in such horrendous pain? Right or wrong, more than anything, I wished it would end.

I focused on the door, hoping perhaps that I could conjure someone upstairs, that if I willed it hard enough, I could bewitch one of my siblings up onto the landing to save me.

Surely, they would realise that by now I should be eating my rice crispies? *Pop, pop, pop.* Tyson would be wondering where I was. As I stared, I saw diagonally across the landing, the figure of a woman in a long, old-fashioned dress. She was startlingly clear; the ruffles on her dress were so detailed and her eyes shone with a kindness which touched my heart. I just wasn't used to such tenderness. She didn't speak and neither did I. But her face was calm and peaceful, and I reached out, through my mind, towards her.

When Dad was finished with me, he slung his arm across me and to my horror, he began to snore. I was trapped under the weight of his arm; him, thick set and heavy, with a neck as wide as his head, me slight and small, even for my age. Much as I was frightened of disturbing him, I was also fearful of missing school, and slowly, very slowly, I inched out, from under his grasp, like a circus performer, along the mattress, until I was able to drop, silently, onto the carpet.

Like a little robot, I went through my morning routine, patting the dogs, pouring my cereal, hunting through laundry to find a pair of matching socks. But I could not ignore the stinging between my legs. I could still smell the stale sweat from his armpits. I could hear his snores, drilling into my brain.

Sitting in class that morning, I didn't think about the attack. I didn't even try not to think about it. I just shut down and I thought about nothing. Instead, I concentrated on writing my capital letters over and over again; A, A, A, B, B, B, C…

"Lovely work," smiled my teacher. "You can have one of my gold stars, Patricia."

But I didn't want a gold star. I didn't want to be praised, just as I didn't want to be disciplined. I didn't want to be under the spotlight for any reason at all; good or bad. At playtime, at home-time, at bedtime, I stayed silent about the abuse. I didn't tell anyone. Not, primarily, because I was protecting my father, but because I didn't know what to say, or who to tell. I had no idea what had happened to me because I didn't even know if something *had* actually happened. And so for me, for now at least, there was no dilemma.

****

Two days on, it was a Saturday, and I woke early, as usual, but there was the luxury of knowing I didn't have to hurry through my morning and get myself out to school. I was making my way across the landing when, to my dismay, I heard my father's voice.

"Tricia," he said firmly. "In here. Now."

My heart stuttered a little. He could have been calling me in to open the curtains for him. Or to find him a pair of socks. Maybe he was about to announce we were going swimming. There were so many scenarios swirling around my brain and, as I edged into the room, I clung hopefully to each one in the same way I clutched at dandelion clocks floating on the breeze. But from the sound of his voice, from the way he cleared his throat, I just knew.

"Yes?" I squeaked, my voice barely a whisper.

Dad didn't reply and instead patted the space next to him, in the bed. Impatiently at first, and then, almost angrily. As

if this was what I deserved. A punishment for some misde-
meanour I was yet to make. Gingerly, I climbed into the bed
and laid my head on the pillow.

Lying there, next to my father, in that big, comfy bed with
the floral duvet cover and the plump pillows should have
been such a treat. The scene should have been synonymous
with comfort and security. Instead, I lay quivering, stiff with
anticipation, my hands by my side, my fingers digging into
the flesh on my legs, through my pyjamas.

Dad seemed in no hurry this morning; perhaps because it
was Saturday, perhaps because watching me squirm was all
part of the plan, all part of his gratification. He grunted and
grumbled a little, and part of me dared to hope he had just
asked me in here to watch cartoons on TV, after all.

There was a small TV at the end of their bed, but it was
switched off. The only other TV in the house was downstairs in the living room. Yet, as I stared at the blank screen,
I knew I would not be watching any television. The waiting
was torture. I wasn't used to keeping so quiet and so still, and
the thought of what might be coming next filled me with
absolute dread.

"Come here," Dad ordered, pulling me over to his pillow.

And then, it began. It was the same as the days before; Dad
pleasuring himself and touching me down below. I didn't
dare object. Just as I would never have dared speak out about
him kicking Tyson or shouting at my friends. To me, this was
another item on a long list of 'Things I Had To Put Up With
From Dad'.

When I looked towards the door, there she was; the lady

with the long flouncy dress and the compassionate face. Normally, like most kids, I was scared of ghosts. But I wanted to run to her, to hide in the folds of her skirts, to feel her arms leading me away to safety. She did not speak. But I knew, from her eyes, that she wanted to help me.

When he was finished, Dad again fell asleep almost immediately, his arm, like a long fat veiny slab of ham, thrown over me and skewering me to the bed. I had no valid reason to sneak out today; I didn't have school. Yet I didn't want to be stuck here until he awoke. I got wafts of his foul breath every time I turned my head, and I could smell that same awful soaked-in stink of sweat. Without making a sound, which I was fast learning was my particular talent in life, I slid slowly out from under his arm and away from his grasp. Within a few seconds, I was scampering down the stairs to safety, hoping there might be some milk left over for my breakfast.

* * * *

The sexual abuse from my father became part of my morning routine, and whilst I hated it, I also accepted it was one of those things I could do nothing about. Dad didn't make a big deal about it, and so neither did I. Aged six, I didn't realise it was bad or wrong. I just knew I really didn't like it. But then, much of my childhood concerned things I really didn't like.

As the months passed, the situation grew steadily worse in parallel and equally horrific ways. Dad made me touch him sexually, and his touching of me became more invasive and more painful. I was subjected also to oral sexual assaults, which I abhorred but could do nothing about. There was no conversation, no communication between us. Dad never explained himself, beyond his anthemic:

"It's not my fault," and "Don't tell anyone. You know I don't like prison."

But I didn't need any kind of explanation. I could recognise the evil. There was a foul stench within him that went far beyond stale smoke and sweat. And in the gloom of those early mornings, his sunken black eyes were as dark as his rotten soul.

Sometimes, hearing the hub-bub downstairs, I would silently wish and plead for one of my siblings, or my mother, to come upstairs to rescue me. Even to just stand at the bottom of the stairs and shout my name.

'Tricia! Get a move on! You're late for school!'

That would have been something, enough, perhaps, to distract my father, to unsettle him, to make him let me go. Occasionally, the odd snippet of sound floated up the stairs and into the bedroom:

'Pop up that toast, it's burning!'

'No, that's my calculator. Give it here. I need it.'

'Has anyone fed the bloody dogs?'

When I was actually in the midst of them, those mornings were so chaotic, they made my head spin. But now, the phrases sounded familiar, endearing almost, and I longed to be a part of it all. They were so completely at odds with the terror I was enduring. It seemed impossible that this was all taking place in the same house. But incredibly, these two situations continued in tandem, month after month after miserable month.

Downstairs was a scene of domestic pandemonium; bickering teenagers, a dining table littered with cereal boxes, homework splattered with toast crumbs, barking dogs and the background whir of the washing machine. It could have been any home in any town, and I marvelled at the ordinariness of it all.

Yet upstairs, only a few metres away, disguised as a parent in a pink bedroom, there lurked an unspeakable evil: A father sexually abusing his own six-year-old daughter, in his own bed, with the door slightly but significantly open, as though he was beyond challenge or reproach. Which of course he was. Even if anyone had discovered his sordid little secret, they would never have dared confront him. And if I was bring honest, if it had been one of the others and I had stumbled upon them, then I, shamefully, would have run away too. I would never have been able to stand up to my father.

Our household was so disjointed and dysfunctional, it had turned each of us inward. Instead of looking out for each other, we all had our own form of tunnel vision, and we looked out only for ourselves. The only witness to my childhood horror was the ghost in the long dress. She could offer me nothing more than a kind look. I knew even then that she was a ghost; she was transparent, and I could see right through her. But I focussed on her face regardless, as though she was a dear friend, a saviour and a protector. For she was all I had.

5

Bribery

On November 5, 1994, I celebrated my 7th birthday. As was the pattern of the last couple of years, I got a small box of fireworks as my gift from my parents, and that night as darkness fell, we gathered in the garden where my dad lit a taper and let them all off in quick succession.

Scattered across the muddy patch of grass were assorted parts of broken bikes with popped tyres and snapped chains. And at the top corner of the garden was a dilapidated little shed, with a leaky felt roof, where Floppy, Thumper and Popsy, and Po and Lala lived.

I had been quite looking forward to the firework display, but the bangs were so loud and scary, I ran into the house in terror before the first rocket had even finished. Cowering under the dining table, with Tyson and Bonnie, I clapped my hands over my ears every time a banger went screaming into the night air. Nobody seemed to notice I was missing, less still care that my birthday present had been a spectacular fail.

"You're an ungrateful little shit," my dad grunted when he spotted me under the table with the dogs after the fireworks were done. "I spend good money on fireworks, and you don't even come outside to appreciate them."

I felt his temper rising, like mercury, and I remained perfectly still, my eyes cast downwards, focussing on the stains on the cracked kitchen linoleum. Dad swore and kicked out at the dogs for good measure. I took his bad humour as a good sign, because I had started to notice, prior to each incident of abuse, he would be a bit nicer to me.

Dad quite often sat on the sofa and ate chocolates, never sharing with anyone, despite six hungry pairs of eyes devouring the scene. But one evening, he called me into the living room and said:

"Here Tricia, have some chocolate."

I was so stunned, I forgot to say thank you. He might just as well have offered me a million pounds. His generosity was so out of character, it came with a neon warning, a blaring horn, and I knew it spelled trouble. Dad had a large bar of chocolate in his hand and he broke a chunk off and held it out. Unfortunately, it was dark chocolate, which I didn't like; it was far too sharp for my palate. My own favourites were Turkish Delights, which I was hardly ever allowed. I ate the dark chocolate anyway, to try to appear grateful. But my insides were churning. Deep down, I just knew what was coming next.

"Thank you," I said timidly.

"You're welcome," Dad said. "You're a good girl."

He smiled and it curdled my insides. I'd have preferred an insult.

The following morning, before school, he called me into the bedroom, on my way past, and sexually abused me before I went downstairs for breakfast. I thought back to the square of dark chocolate; a bribe which had been so bitter, I had struggled to swallow it. I understood now that the blockage in my throat had nothing to do with the taste.

Another time, the 'pop man' had been round, a regular on our estate, with his crates of cream soda and dandelion and burdock. We were not allowed to help ourselves, but Dad called me into the kitchen and nodded at the glass bottles, lined up by the back door.

"Go on, get yourself a drink," he said. "Choose whichever one you want."

Much as this was an unprecedented treat, I felt my heart dropping like a stone. Tentatively, I half-filled a glass and sipped at the drink, dreading what it foreshadowed.

The next morning was a Sunday. I stayed in bed as long as I could, hoping Dad might get tired of waiting for me and go downstairs, to the sofa, or even out of the house. But the moment I swung my legs out of bed, I was conscious of his presence. I knew he was in the house – in his bedroom – without even checking. I crept along the landing so quietly, sucking my breath in, but it was useless.

"Tricia!" he called. "Tricia, is that you?"

My insides liquefied each time I heard his voice. Every bone in my body revolted.

'No, No, No. Don't go in there.'

But I went in. I had to. It was like I was magnetised, and he reeled me in just as if I was one of the little fish in Bluebell Woods.

There you go little fish, back with your mummy and daddy…

I was trapped in a strange cycle of bribes, punishments and abuse and there was no way out. When Dad was angry, I at least knew where I was with him. When he was nice, then it really was time for me to worry.

Sometimes, Dad's approach was far less prosaic than a bribe with chocolate or fizzy pop. I could intuit an attack simply from a half smile or even a slight change in his tone of voice. These subtle signs of benevolence spelled danger for me. A smile in the evening usually led to an attack the following morning. I am unsure, looking back, whether this sense of hypervigilance existed before the sexual abuse, or whether it was simply sharpened and heightened by it.

I do not know whether I became so painfully aware of my father's moods as a form of self-preservation, or whether it was simply an over-sensitivity that I was born with. Regardless, it really didn't help me at all and in fact it was probably a huge hindrance. Knowing he was about to blow his stack, or knowing I was about to be abused, was not useful. I could not escape either his temper or his perversions. I simply learned to anticipate and dread them in advance, and sometimes, the dread was worse even than the deed itself.

In the run up to Christmas 1994, around a year after the abuse began, I saw a TV advert for a doll called Baby Expressions. She made real baby sounds, and her eyes and mouth opened and closed so she could drink from a bottle or even suck a dummy. She cried like a baby kitten when she was laid down and her chest rose and fell softly as though she was actually breathing. My eyes grew wide with longing each time I saw the advert.

"Oh, I'd love a Baby Expressions," I sighed. "I really would."

Lisa had asked for the same doll for Christmas too. We wrote letters to Santa in class at school, and Baby Expressions was at the top of every list. I was young enough to believe in Santa and in the magic of Christmas, but with a sharp pinch of reality added into the mix. And even then, as I posted my list, off to Lapland, I knew I had absolutely no chance of getting the doll. Little girls like me didn't get fancy dolls like that.

One year, I got a second-hand Barbie horse and carriage, which delighted me. Despite the scuffs and a wonky wheel, I got lots of fun out of it. The toy I played with most though was a snooker table I'd made myself, from cardboard, complete with small snooker balls, made of scrunched paper, and old biros as cues. I wasn't used to brand new or extravagant toys.

On Christmas morning, still dreamily imagining myself cradling Baby Expressions as she cried in my arms, I came down to breakfast along with all the others. We followed the usual routine, obediently eating breakfast whilst we craned our necks to see the Christmas tree, through the archway, to size up the presents underneath. My gift was inside a large parcel wrapped in shiny red. And as I ripped off the paper, after breakfast, I gasped in astonishment. I could hardly believe my eyes. There, staring back at me with her uncannily life-like eyes, was a Baby Expressions. A real one! It was brand new too, still in the box.

"Look!" I yelled, dancing around the living room. "A Baby Expressions! I got it! Hurray! My own baby!"

It was confirmation for me that Santa was absolutely 100% real. That no matter what atrocities I endured the other 364 days of the year, he'd always make it all alright for me in the end. I loved my doll, and I cherished her as though she was a real baby.

I presumed 'Expressions' was her exotic Christian name and I never saw any need to change it. I was maternal, even as a little girl, and I took my duties very seriously. She had a packet of miniature nappies, and I was at first fascinated by the way she finished a bottle of formula and then weed into her nappy. But when it came time to take off her nappy, for a new one, I got a sudden sickly feeling. It didn't feel right, somehow, taking off her pants and putting on a new nappy. I couldn't explain it. I just didn't feel it was the right thing to do.

Baby Expressions stared back at me as I paused, with the nappy in my hand, my face creased into a frown. Her eyes were blank, her pink mouth fixed into a small smile. Like me, her true feelings were masked. Her suffering was hidden. Like the over-developed sensitivity which predicted my father's attacks, I felt strongly and inexplicably it was not the right thing for me to take off her nappy. With a heavy heart, and not understanding why, I put the nappy back in the packet. I could not put her through it. Or perhaps I could not put myself through it.

"Sorry Baby Expressions," I said gently. "I'll change it next time, I promise."

After bathing and feeding, I took her out with me, pushing an old dolls' pram, whilst Tyson and Bonnie trotted obediently at my side, around the estate. I was so proud of her.

"Good girl, Baby Expressions," I cooed. "You have a little sleep. Mummy is here."

Now, I look back at the relative expense and extravagance, so out of the ordinary for my father, and I wonder whether the doll was his idea of a sick Christmas trade-off. A way of keeping me quiet; the fulcrum of an unholy alliance. She was a gift, not from Santa, but from Satan.

6

The Stained Glass Window

Into the New Year of 1995, the abuse continued with a stomach-turning regularity. It was always the same routine; in the mornings, in his bedroom, with the door open, involving invasive and painful touching. And as the weeks passed, the abuse grew steadily worse. Dad forced me to touch him more and more and to perform sex acts on him. I felt myself gagging, not just at the act itself but at the smell also.

Some mornings, he would make me undress completely, then stand at the side of the bed and bend over whilst he masturbated. I loathed it. It was awkward and uncomfortable, and I felt so exposed and vulnerable. Again, I heard the odd bicycle, or kids on scooters, passing below. I heard people walking past the window, chatting and laughing. And I wondered how it could be that the normal world was so near and yet so very, very far away. It ran through my mind that I could, improbably, call out to the people below:

"Help me! Rescue me!"

But from what? I was in a bedroom, in my own home, with my own father. I didn't know how to explain what was wrong. What would they rescue me from – and to? In desperation, as I was bent over, I craned my neck towards the door and sure enough, there she was, my guardian ghoul, watching over me, her eyes shining with mercy and humanity.

I wanted so much to hear her voice, for her to cry out and tell my father to stop. She would know how to explain it, she would know what to do. But a part of me was frightened, too; wary of her speaking up and annoying my father. Would I get the blame for a ghost telling him off? Would any intervention, even of the divine kind, just make him even worse? Probably, yes.

Dad rarely spoke whilst it was happening. Beyond perfunctory commands; touch this, bend here, do that, he said very little. His breathing was loud and laboured and often I felt a fine spray of spittle on the back of my neck. When it was over, his face would crease with worry. His voice trembled as he spoke, and I did not know whether it was with anger or with fear:

"Don't tell anyone, Tricia. You know this isn't my fault. I'm just made this way. I'll go to prison, and you know how much I hate prison."

It was a peculiar statement. I never thought to ask him how he knew he hated prison or indeed if he had ever been to prison. But such was the ferocity and frequency of his plea that I grew up with a morbid fear of going to prison myself.

To this day, I have never broken the law, yet I am still petrified, irrationally so, of ending up behind bars. As well as being frightened of my father, I was also scared of the dark. At night, in bed, when all the lights were off, I'd often wish I could see the friendly ghost, to cheer me up. I'd close my eyes and try to conjure her up somehow, with a wish.

"Come on, Mrs Ghost," I whispered. "Where are you?"

Opening and closing my eyes a few times rapidly, I hoped she might be there to surprise me. I fancied I could hear the rustle of her skirts, I believed I could see her pallid face, white in the darkness. But I was tricking myself. She never came to me at night; she was only ever there during the abuse. There when I needed her most.

* * * *

One morning, in the early months of 1995, I woke with a bit of a winter cold. Dad must have heard me coughing during the night, because he came to the bedroom door and said:

"Day off for you Tricia, I think. You don't sound well to me."

This would normally have been wonderful news. Like any child, I loved having a sneaky day off school. But I was instantly mistrustful. Just like the dark chocolate, just like the cream soda, I could smell a stinking rat. I was never allowed a day off school. I remembered being sent in regardless, once even when I'd vomited after breakfast. So to keep me off sick when I had nothing worse than a sniffle was very suspicious and disconcerting.

"Ok, Dad," I replied cautiously.

The house soon emptied out; the older ones went to school and work. Mum was working a double shift. Soon it was just Dad and I left.

"You watch TV if you like," he told me casually. "Go on. Into the living room. I'll join you."

Again, the alarm bells clanged loudly in my head. This just was not like Dad. Not at all. He was being nice, and I knew how dangerous that was. Gingerly, I made my way downstairs, with my Baby Expressions under my arm, and I switched the telly on. I perched on an armchair and Dad followed and took up his usual position lying across the sofa. Even with the TV on, the house felt unusually, spookily, quiet.

I couldn't remember ever being at home, watching TV, just with Dad, by myself. On the surface, I fixed my eyes on the TV screen and pretended to be absorbed in a daytime cookery show. But inside, the panic coursed through me, out of control, ripping at my insides. I was gripped by a nebulous yet very distinct aura of menace, almost as strong as a premonition. I could feel it. I could taste it. I could hear it, screeching in my ears. But what was it?

At the edge of my vision, I was aware Dad was standing up and walking towards my chair. The scene slowed right down, it took an age each time he lifted a leg for it to hit the ground again, as though he was walking on the moon. The smallest movement was amplified. Everything mattered more.

"Get undressed," he ordered.

My whole body tensed in protest. But I stood up and did exactly as he said.

"Bend over."

Once again, I did exactly as he said. I had no other choice.

"Keep still."

My knees were shaking, my teeth were chattering and every bone in my body was trembling, but I concentrated really hard on trying to stay still.

There was a panel of stained-glass in the living room door and I focussed on the panel, and on the patterns and colours in the glass, and hoped I could soon stand up and it would be over. But in the next moment I felt the most horrific pain as if I was being torn in two. Dad had always warned me to be quiet during the abuse, but I couldn't help screaming out. I felt a meaty hand clamp over my mouth as the tears streamed silently, pointlessly, down my face and through his thick, yellow fingers. Still I stared at the door, wishing it would open, praying someone might come and save me. The coloured glass flickered with the light from the television and, as the agony seared through me, I made myself recite the colours:

'Red, yellow, green. Yellow again.'

I heard Dad zipping up his trousers. At last, it was over; physically, at least.

"Come here," he said. "Let me look at you. Check there's no damage."

To my horror, he insisted on an intimate examination, making sure there was no evidence of what he had done.

My knees could barely hold me up; I had never experienced pain or terror like it.

"Right, you can get dressed now." he said. Again, it was his matter-of-fact voice; he might just as well have been checking my head for lice or looking at a verruca on my foot.

"And remember, you don't tell anyone. And I mean it. None of this is my fault."

He was unconcerned by my discomfort and my trauma. His only worry was he might have left behind damning proof of his own depravity. A small whimpering noise slipped from my lips, and Dad snarled:

"Put a sock in it, Tricia. Nobody likes a whiner."

He left the room, and I collapsed back onto the chair, faint and dizzy with distress. I could not move; I was screwed to the seat, as if there was a metal stake right through me. Squeezing my eyes closed, I felt a sudden and powerful wind shooting through me, and it picked me up like a scrap of litter and buffeted me all around the room, whirling me round and round, until most of my insides were shaken out and lost. By the time I was dropped carelessly back onto the chair, I was without substance or solidity. I was a mere outline, a wobbly pencil drawing of my old self. That night, in bed, I wept quietly.

'None of this is my fault'

Dad's words ran round and round my mind like trapped rats. If it wasn't his fault then logically, it had to be mine. There were only two of us there. What had I done to deserve such misery?

Only then, in the lonely darkness, I realised my ghost lady

hadn't been there for me, in the living room. There was nobody there for me. Not even a figment of my imagination. Even she had deserted me when I needed her the most. I was totally alone.

* * * *

I eventually cried myself to sleep but awoke, still sobbing, at intervals during the night. The next morning, feeling nauseous and sore, I was, ironically, too ill for school. But today, I was made to go in. It was not an issue for negotiation. Nobody cared when I actually was ill. Hobbling along the pavement, I could barely walk; I was in so much pain down below.

7

An Unexpected Illness

"Are you OK?" one of the school-run mums asked. "You look a bit pale, Patricia and you seem to be limping. Have you hurt yourself, darling?"

For some reason, her unexpected kindness brought a lump to my throat, and I couldn't find any words. I just shrugged and shuffled off without replying. That night, my older siblings were home, and they too noticed I wasn't myself.

"I'm really sore," I told them shyly. "Down below. I don't know why."

I didn't connect the soreness with the attack, and so didn't realise I was supposed to keep quiet about it. I even complained to one of my brothers over our evening meal.

"I can't sit down, it's so sore," I said. "You know, my thingy."

"Maybe you should see the doctor," my brother frowned. "Doesn't sound right to me. Might be a urine infection, what do you think, Dad?"

"She's just dramatic," Dad snapped. "Silly little cow. Shut up Tricia, you're doing my head in with your moaning. Nobody likes a whiner. I've told you that before."

And so that was that. I did as I was told, and I shut myself up.

* * * *

A couple of weeks after the attack in the living room, I was walking up the stairs, with my Baby Expressions in my arms, taking care to avoid the carpet tracking with my bare feet. We'd had no carpet in the hallway or on the stairs for months and I had scars on the soles of my feet to prove it. There was a half-way turn on our stairs, and I paused, briefly, to give Baby Expressions her dummy and rock her a little.

"It's OK baby," I whispered. "Mummy's here. You're going up for a bottle and a bath."

I was about to carry on, round the corner and up the last few stairs, to my bedroom, when I felt myself go groggy and dizzy. When I opened an eye it was on a level with a dusty skirting board and a scrap of curling wallpaper.

"Tricia! Tricia?" said my father. "What are you doing?"

My mother's voice was in the background, on the phone, calling an ambulance.

"Stay where you are," she said. "The paramedics are on their way."

My thought processes were foggy and fragmented, but I knew I'd had Baby Expressions in my arms a moment ago, and now she was gone. I wanted to ask for her, check if she was alright, but I had such a throbbing pain in my head that it blocked out all other thoughts. I couldn't bear to even lift my head just an inch from the floor. I had extreme brain freeze, as though I'd eaten 10 ice-lollies, one after the other. I could not verbalise a single thought and instead, I just stared up at my father, from the floor, in wide-eyed and silent confusion.

"What's going on?" he demanded again.

Sometime later, it could have been a few minutes or several hours, my grasp of time felt so fragile – there was a knock at the door. I felt a foot shoving me aside, as though I was an inconvenient bag of rubbish.

"You're in the way," my father was grumbling. "I can't get to the door."

The paramedics must have squeezed into the hallway somehow because I was soon sitting up, telling them my name, and my age, and managing to ask for my Baby Expressions.

"We're going to take you to hospital, just to get you checked out," they explained.

I didn't want to go anywhere without my doll, but I didn't dare ask again. Dad's great shadow loomed over me, and I had an inexplicable impression of his temper coming to the boil, as though he might bubble over at any moment. I was carried into the ambulance by the paramedics and went on my own to the hospital. The nurses made such a fuss of me and found me a nice bed and a nightie.

"Lovely to see you again, Patricia," they smiled.

I was used to being in hospital, it didn't bother me at all, and my main concern was how much I was missing my doll, left behind at home on her own.

"What about her bath time?" I fretted.

I was beginning to remember slivers of what had happened directly before my fall, and I had been on my way upstairs, to get her pyjamas from my bedroom and then take her to the bathroom. And of course, after her bath, she liked a bottle and a nap in her pram. Who would take care of her, now I was gone?

"Can I go home later?" I asked.

The nurse looked doubtful.

"You had a fall on the stairs," she told me. "Do you remember that? Do you remember how you felt before you fell? Were you ill? Or sick? Any pains before you blacked out?"

I shook my head uncertainly. I wasn't sure I really recalled anything at all about the fall itself. My head still throbbed. I had a big purple bruise blooming on my leg and an imprint of the carpet tracking on my shin.

"I think you'll be with us for a few days," she told me. "The porter will be along soon to take you for a brain scan."

My mouth fell open in shock and I temporarily forgot about Baby Expressions.

"A scan of my brain?" I asked in awe.

The nurse smiled.

"It's nothing to worry about," she reassured me.

But I was deeply concerned. What if the scanner read my

thoughts? I did not use foul language out loud, but I heard enough of it at home. And suddenly I became panicked that all the naughty words I knew would flood into my brain and be somehow relayed onto the scanner. I'd get into so much trouble if I was caught swearing. I imagined my teacher's disappointed face. I pictured my father's anger. I envisaged my siblings sniggering and teasing me. Oh, this was exactly the kind of attention I spent my life trying to avoid. And what about the horrible things Dad did to me? My mind flashed back to the stained-glass door, the ghost lady, the big, sweaty arm pinning me down.

'Don't tell anyone, Tricia. This is not my fault. I don't want to go to prison.'

What if these scrappy memories barged uninvited, into my brain, right at the moment the machine was reading my mind? Dad would explode. Beyond furious. And what if I was responsible for sending him to prison? I had only a vague idea of what prison was, but I knew there was a link between the abuse and prison, and I understood Dad was adamant he didn't want to go.

The responsibility was crushing me, just like his big arm, and the pain in my head pounded and pounded. By the time the porter came to take me to the X-ray department, I was shaking with fear.

"Don't worry, it's a scan, it doesn't hurt at all," said the nurse briskly. "You'll be back here soon. No need to get upset."

She was right, of course. The procedure was completely painless, and I tried, with all my might, to clear my mind and focus only on my Baby Expressions and the way her chest rose and fell, when I lay her down, just like a real baby.

I tried to think of Tyson and Bonnie and the way their tails wagged at the front window when they saw me walking home from school. Tyson had a comical trick of diving straight through one of our lower kitchen windows; he could push the latch open and just land in the middle of the room, unannounced. It always made me giggle. As the scanner hummed gently, I played that scene over and over in my mind, imagining myself laughing and patting his back. Surely these thoughts would be allowed by the scanner?

I half-expected to receive a written transcript of my brain activity, after the scan was finished, with all the swear words in red capital letters, but I was wheeled back to the ward, and into bed, and I was none the wiser.

Later that evening, visiting time started, and I had no visitors. I was used to that but a small part of me still longed, in a parallel universe, for my devoted father to arrive, carrying a box of Turkish Delight and a can of my favourite cream soda, with Baby Expressions under his arm, exclaiming at how brave I was and how much he had missed me. But this was my reality and there was nobody.

The little girl in the next bed to me had a broken leg, and her parents turned up carrying a large cardboard box. When she opened it, a bunch of helium balloons floated out into the ward. It was magical, like a fairground stall, right there, in her bed. Seeing me staring, enviously transfixed, her mother took one of the balloons and brought it over for me.

"Here," she smiled. "You take this. Cassie has plenty."

"Thank you!" I beamed.

I tied the balloon, which was a shiny purple, onto my headboard and leaned back with a contented smile. I had a visitor after all! I had a gift! I drifted off to sleep, with my headache easing, dreaming of Baby Expressions.

* * * *

Two days later, my father came to collect me from the hospital.

"We think Patricia possibly had an epileptic fit," the doctor explained. "The scan at this point is inconclusive. Is there any family history of epilepsy?"

My father shook his head.

"And has she had any traumatic events, any undue stress that you can think of?"

Again, my father shook his head, this time with complete authority. I remained silent. I knew better than to chirp up with my opinion. Besides, for me, aged seven, my recent trauma was not a violent sexual assault. My recent trauma was being separated from my beloved doll. I had no concept of the gravity of the sexual abuse. I had no concept at all of sexual abuse. And the fact that the doctor was asking my own abuser about my own emotional health, just compounded and confused the issue even more in my mind.

We'd like to see her again in the clinic next week," the doctor continued. "We've started her on daily medication, and this can continue at home. Any problems before then, anything you're worried about, please bring her straight back."

I was very relieved to have escaped without any punishment from the mind-reading brain scanner. And I was so looking forward to getting home to my doll and my dogs.

In the car, on the journey home, Dad didn't speak. He didn't even look at me. Yet I could feel it, like a storm cloud rolling over a distant hill, like a slight scratch in the back of my throat, signalling the onset of a nasty virus. I knew it was coming.

At the final junction, before we turned into the estate for home, he leaned and put his hand on my bare leg, high enough up my thigh to touch my underwear. Instinctively, I recoiled, ever so slightly, hoping it wasn't enough to get me into trouble. But Dad didn't take his eyes off the road. He continued driving, replaced his hand on the steering wheel, and that was the end of it. For now. Just for now. I realised I was just as repelled by what might have been as I was by the abuse itself.

8

Home Sick

I was not always aware of the seizures themselves. Sometimes I'd find myself staring blankly into space and then I heard someone calling my name, far away, in the dusty recesses of my mind. I tried to reply, but the distance was too great, and I could never shout back loud enough. Other times, I might feel nothing more than a slight tingling in my arms and legs. Afterwards, I had the most awful headaches, always as though I'd crunched through a box of ice lollies in record-breaking time. But mostly, I had no symptoms at all.

My worst seizure was falling on the stairs that day; there had been nothing as serious since. My days slid one into the other; a mixed-up mess of abuse, epileptic fits and hospital appointments. Dad woke me one morning and said abruptly:

"You have a bump on your head. You must have had a fit in the night. You need a day off school."

Sure enough, I had a small bruise on my forehead, but it

was only painful when I pressed it. I had no idea where it had come from, only that it had not been there when I went to bed. And I really did not want a day off school. I associated days off sick with a sadness inside and a soreness down below. But I could not think of a way round it.

Not once, ever, did I think of standing up to my father or confronting him. When he was calling me into his bedroom, to be abused, I didn't dare come up with an excuse, or fabricate a reason, why he should just leave me alone and let me be. It was unthinkable to speak out against him, or even merely to suggest it. I felt guilty for thinking it. So when Dad informed me I'd had a fit, and told me I had to stay off school, I just agreed with him mutely.

"I'll call school," he told me. "You can't go in. No way."

That morning I stayed in bed as long as I could, before hunger got the better of me and I crept downstairs to find some cereal. Dad was in the living room, with the television on, and when I peeped round the door, he was quite openly masturbating. Later, I realised he was watching pornography on the telly, but at the time, it just seemed like a lot of naked people making a strange noise to me. It was intriguing and vaguely disturbing, and even a little bit amusing.

"Here you are," Dad grunted belligerently, as if I was late for something. "Get yourself upstairs. Into my bed. Now."

My breakfast would have to wait. I turned and felt him behind me, on the stairs, and quickened my step. I wanted this over with; done. Forgotten. Yet I didn't want it to begin. I wanted it pushed as far into the future as it would go. Simultaneously, I wanted time to accelerate and to rewind.

My mind was such a tangle of emotions, racing round faster and faster. It was only when it began, and my faithful ghost appeared at the door, that my heart slowed a little. She was shimmering and in parts brilliantly white, in other parts completely transparent, with the kind face I had come to know and love. She held my gaze until Dad was finished; she brought a strong sensibility of solidarity to my suffering, and it helped immeasurably.

"We need to get you back to the doctor, see about these fits," Dad said, as I got myself dressed. "You can't go to school if you keep having seizures. You're going to have to stay at home with me."

****

Back at the hospital, after hearing Dad's account of my night-time seizure, the doctor prescribed more medication. Already, on the original dose, I was feeling tired and sluggish. These were recognised side-effects of the drugs and I really didn't want any more tablets. I didn't want to feel any worse. But nobody asked me.

"She seems to be fitting mostly during the night," Dad told him. "Tricia doesn't remember them at all. Good job I'm up and about keeping an eye on her. Anything could happen to her."

We were sent home with the new medication and with instructions to return for another check up in a couple of weeks. Over the following days, the new medication kicked in and I felt awful. I was exhausted, even after a good night's sleep, and then nauseous and light-headed all day long. Some evenings, I had splitting headaches, so severe that my vision blurred. I could do nothing but curl up on my bunk bed after school and wait for the pain to ease.

As I lay with my eyes closed, I'd feel a warm nose snuffling my hair and then Tyson gently laid his head on mine. It was as though he knew I had a headache; he had a hyper-vigilance, a sensitivity for pain and upset, just like me. The thought made me love him all the more.

"Thanks Ty," I whispered. "We're the same, you and me. You're the only medicine I need."

The medication stifled my appetite too. Even though I was thin, and I was constantly being told I needed to eat more, there were days when I couldn't stomach food. It took a supreme effort to force down a few rice crispies before school each morning.

Tyson stared up at me in concern, his big brown eyes filled with worry as I sobbed, silently, into my cereal bowl. He whimpered quietly as I stumbled out of the kitchen, and off to school. But nobody else seemed to notice.

Mainly, I had minor seizures known as absences, where I might find myself blinking rapidly, or staring into space, unable to focus. I'd have pins and needles in my arms and legs, and I had big, floaty, multi-coloured shapes poking around the edges of my vision. There were hexagons of all colours. Each one, jabbing at my eyeline, felt like a physical assault. And always, afterwards, I had that horrible feeling of regret at having eaten too much ice cream or too many ice lollies.

I was so tired, and all I wanted to do each morning was go back to bed and sleep. But no matter how weary I was, I couldn't risk requesting a day off school. Anything was better than finding myself alone at home with my father. I had no choice but to push on, to somehow drag myself out of the house and down the path. My loyal Tyson came to the door and watched me leave with a mournful face, as though he was trying to tell me I really should have been tucked up in bed.

"Bye Tyson," I said miserably. "I'll be back later."

Taking him and Bonnie for an afternoon walk around the estate drained the last dregs of energy from me, it was like wringing a dry dishcloth. But though they were physically depleting, those walks gave me an emotional boost. I downloaded all my worries and my complaints onto Tyson as we walked, and he gave me wise and encouraging nods in reply.

"I hate this medicine. I feel sick all the time. I don't even know what epileptic fits are. Do you Tyson? Do I look epileptic to you? No, I didn't think so."

He maintained a sensible silence, which I took to mean he was firmly on my side. And when my voice wavered, with the threat of tears, he stopped and nuzzled his nose into my palm.

"I know," I said gratefully, wiping my cheeks with my sleeve. "I know you love me, Ty."

The next week, back at the hospital, the doctors decided my medication was too strong and it was reduced a little. But then Dad reminded them I'd had more fits since my last appointment.

"I'm not sure you should be reducing the dosage," he said tetchily. "She's not ready for this."

There was some discussion between him and the doctor whilst I stared at my hands on my lap. Then Dad said:

"I want to apply for a payment from the Family Fund. Do you think Tricia might qualify? With her being so unwell?"

There was more discussion which I didn't fully understand. But it turned out Dad was intending to apply for a pay-out from a charitable fund, set up to help the families of sick children at the hospital. Of course, to do that, he needed a sick child. And that was where I came in, handily enough. On this occasion, the doctor, unfortunately, didn't think I was quite ill enough for him to recommend Dad for the fund.

"I'm sorry, Mr King," he said. "I can't support your request."

I knew, before Dad even spoke, that he was livid. His eyes were sinking into his face, as if they were being swallowed up into a crevasse. His jaw was tightly clenched. He was wrestling to keep his temper in check, in front of the doctor. I was anxious, on behalf of the doctor, on behalf of myself, and I felt myself going clammy and jittery. There was an itch around my neckline; a tell-tale sign of a red rash which ran across my skin, spider-like, when I was agitated. I pulled at my collar, but it didn't help, and I felt the rash moving resolutely towards my cheeks.

"Well, maybe we'll qualify next time," Dad said shortly, standing up and glaring at me to do the same. "I really hope so. I think it's only fair for you to assess us again soon. You know how many seizures she has. And then there's her asthma. And her tummy troubles. If we don't qualify for a payment, who the hell does?"

He marched out down the hospital corridor, and I had to run to try and keep pace. As he walked, his anger with the doctor was somehow transferred onto me, and when he reached the main doors, a few seconds before me, he yelled:

"Come on Tricia! Stop dawdling. I'm sick of it. Just do as you're told and keep up."

It's difficult for me to be sure, as an adult, just how severe my childhood fits were. Certainly, I had two memorable seizures and several instances, which could have been potential absences, where I drifted off, momentarily. But I do not remember having fits every week, or even every day, as my father insisted. And later medical records would show there was little evidence to back up his claims too.

It wasn't even proven I definitely had epilepsy. It's far more likely, as I look back, that the fits were trauma-induced, triggered by the sexual abuse. And so, aged 7, I found myself in the intolerable position where the person who was responsible for my illness was also my carer for that same illness. With such an arrangement, I was unlikely ever to make a full recovery, or any progress at all.

Perhaps Dad was exaggerating my illness because he wanted a pay out from the hospital's Family Fund. Or maybe my illness suited him because it gave him a straightforward, cast-iron reason to keep me off school, so he could sexually abuse me, in an empty house, without fear of being discovered or interrupted.

Another possibility is he had an undiagnosed and twisted

form of Munchausen syndrome by proxy, where he was intent on being the parent of a very sick child; for the attention, the money, the sympathy, the drama… Who knows? My guess is the answers probably lie in none yet all of these scenarios, and his thought processes were an evil mix of the whole lot.

I certainly did have two seizures and I definitely had a medical condition, but I believe the roots of this were psychological. As an adult I've researched Non-Epileptic Attack Disorder (NEAD) where a patient superficially appears to have an epileptic fit but there is in fact no epileptic activity in the brain and the disturbances are instead caused by severe trauma.

Given that my first, and most serious seizure, occurred just after I was seriously sexually assaulted as a child, this would seem to fit perfectly with NEAD. I started bed-wetting around that time too; Dad told the doctors this was because I was having night-time seizures, but equally, and more likely, the incontinence was a consequence of my trauma.

The doctors who treated me at the time knew nothing about the sexual abuse of course, and so the link was never made or even considered, as far I as knew. And, after listening to my father's credible accounts of night-time seizures and recurring absences, I almost began to believe it was true myself. Like most small children, I did not question my father. If my dad told me I had epileptic fits, then I accepted it as the truth. The alternative, that I was being groomed and brainwashed as part of his predatory campaign, was too grotesque and too complex for me to even consider.

Just as with Dad's mood changes, I experienced a prescient

hyper-sensitivity around the fits and I could almost sniff one out, as it wormed its sinister way through my brain towards the surface. I felt sick with foreboding and apprehension as it grew closer and closer. It inched its way through my body, in the same way that the ugly red rash crawled up my neck. Soon, I could predict my seizures, just as I could predict the abuse from Dad.

And perhaps my hyper-vigilance both foreshadowed and encouraged the fits. My anxiety doubtless made me more fearful and nervous than ever, which in turn made me more vulnerable to Dad's attacks, which in turn made me more susceptible to a seizure.

Each of these events seemed to hinge and depend on each other, and also aggravate and exacerbate the other. It was a strange and sickening correlation, and I was never quite sure which was dependent on which. I was never quite sure which came first. But I was quite sure I hated the abuse. I was quite sure I hated the seizures.

9

Fuzzy and Weary

My eighth birthday in November 1995 passed in a shower of frightful fireworks and once again, whilst the family huddled in our muddy back garden, I took up my usual position under the dining table, with Tyson, my furry ally, by my side.

"I know," I whispered, taking his quivering paw in my hand. "I don't like them either. But don't bark. Dad will get cross."

Tyson still had a pink weal across his back from the last time Dad had let loose with the metal end of the dog leash. But he was an irrepressible dog, and whilst the fireworks whistled and screamed, he did a funny little dance, rocking on his front paws, to make me laugh. It was the best moment of my birthday, hiding under the table and watching Tyson dancing. Christmas 1995 passed, and the sexual abuse continued, mostly in Dad's bedroom and usually in the mornings before I went to school.

The horrific incident in the living room was not repeated. At Dad's insistence, I was spending more and more time at home, apparently too unwell to go into school. And with only Dad and I in the house, I felt horribly and agonisingly exposed. Ours was a house which was usually bursting at the seams with people, animals and arguments.

In addition to the eight of us and our menagerie of pets, Dad's father and siblings, who lived a few doors down, often came to visit too. It was a daily challenge to find a place to sit or a quiet spot just to read my book or play with Baby Expressions. I didn't even have my own bedroom. So to have an entire house to ourselves, just Dad and I, should have been wonderfully liberating. Instead, I felt panicky and claustrophobic. I could barely breathe some days, under the stress of waiting for the abuse to start. The silence screamed in my ears.

It became nauseatingly normal and commonplace for me to come back from walking Tyson, or skip into the house from feeding my rabbits, and find Dad watching a pornographic video, right there in the family living room.

"Tricia?" he called. "Don't go out again. I need you in a minute."

At some point, he'd pause the film and order me upstairs, into his bedroom. I never dared even consider refusing him. Nor did I think my father watching pornography was unacceptable, or even out of the ordinary. I had nothing else to compare it to, after all. As with the plagues of nits, I would continue believing this was standard, until I was told otherwise.

This was my home life, and I simply went along with it, because I had no other options. I had no idea if other houses were different to mine. Perhaps all fathers watched pornography in the living room. Maybe all children went through this horrific abuse. How was I to know?

"You tell nobody at all," he always reminded me. "Say nothing about what I watch on telly. Nothing about what goes on in the bedroom. I can't go to prison. You know that."

Ironically, if Dad ever caught me watching cartoons on telly, he pulled no punches.

"No wonder you're thick as shit, you watch such rubbish," he'd say. "Turn that mindless crap off. You're hopeless."

Wounded, I did just as he said. His words stung. Was I really thick as shit? Hopeless? It was true, I was struggling a little at school. But then, I was hardly ever in class. I had so much time off, with sickness and seizures and various illnesses, some less credible than others, and my education was bound to suffer.

Dad didn't seem to like me going to school, he purposely kept me at home when I wanted to go in, and yet he mocked me when I began to fall behind. If it was anyone's fault I was thick and hopeless, surely it was his? But as a child, I didn't see the logic. And I accepted I was to blame, just as I was to blame for everything else.

The mental cruelty was pernicious and, in its own way, was almost as damaging as the sexual abuse. My father battered away at my self-belief, at the very centre of myself, and gradually, his lies soaked through my skin like a poison and I began to believe them. I was thick. I was useless. I was at fault. I felt so miserable, but I kept quiet and waited until I was out with Tyson for our walk to confide in him. He was the best listener I could have asked for.

"I am not as clever as my friends," I told Tyson. "But I'm doing my best. I wish I could go to school every day. I think it might help."

Tyson yapped in agreement. I didn't enjoy school, but I was desperate to go. Anything was better than the hell at home. But if anything, as the months passed, my school attendance just got worse. In one school year I had 71 days off. In another, the term began, the weeks passed, and I just didn't go back. When the teachers called to ask where I was, Dad told them:

"She's a difficult kid. Always ill and she has a lot of issues, you know. There's only so much you do as a parent. I do my best with her."

And so, one of Dad's favourite ways of papering over his own depravity was to deflect the attention and the criticism onto others. If there was ever a news report on TV about paedophilia, he'd explode with an exaggerated rage.

"Disgusting," he'd snap. "They should throw away the key. Bring back hanging. Dirty buggers."

A man we barely knew from our estate was arrested in connection with child sex offences, and Dad ranted about it for weeks. I didn't see his guile or hypocrisy, back then. I didn't know what paedophiles were and I could never have equated them with what happened in Dad's bedroom. But looking back, it is clear to me he was shouting the loudest because he had the most to hide.

****

In parallel with the abuse, my hospital appointments continued. I went through months of trying different types and dosages of medication. It felt as though I'd just got used to taking one drug when it was replaced by another, and I had a constant and unsettling sensation of having a tablet permanently lodged at the back of my throat. No matter how much I drank or swallowed or gargled, I just couldn't dislodge it.

I went through a phase of swallowing very deliberately and loudly, to try to clear the blockage, but because it was in all likelihood a psychological problem, like the seizures, my worrying just made it all worse. And me clearing my throat repeatedly in class did nothing to help me make new friends or endear me to my existing friends. Now, I was the girl who had an odd family, permanent nits, and a very loud swallow.

"Patricia, please be quiet, you're distracting the class," my teacher said, as I gulped my way through the lesson.

A burst of mean laughter rippled through the air, and I hung my head, already feeling a prickling under my shirt collar, and knowing the itchy red rash was the next thing my classmates would revel in sneering at.

I grew to hate the epilepsy drugs and the way they made me feel; it seemed to me they were far more problematic than the seizures themselves. I do understand it's normal to trial different drugs for a newly diagnosed condition. Over the months, I tried Lamotrigine, Tegretol and Carbamazepine. I was prescribed all sorts of different levels and doses, medicines, tablets, solutions. The doctors were just doing their best. But my treatment programme wasn't helped at all by Dad's claims of me having more and more frequent seizures, none of which I could remember, none of which anyone else witnessed, apart from him.

"She's having them during the night again," he told the doctor. "Never at school. Never during the day. But lots at night. She needs stronger medication. She needs more tests."

The doctors wrote to my school to ask how my epilepsy was affecting my education. The teachers replied to say they were not aware of any fits or any side effects, or indeed any problems at all related to seizures. They said the only problem was that I was so rarely in school at all.

"She's never in school because she's so ill," Dad exclaimed.

The doctors never usually asked me for my opinion. I had nothing to add, after all. I had no recollection whatsoever of these fits, but at the same time I had no reason to doubt my father's account. I was too fuzzy and weary with what I thought were the side-effects of my drugs to begin questioning what I was told was my own reality. But one day, a consultant unexpectedly swivelled his chair around to me, and said:

"What do you think, Patricia? How do you feel about trying different drugs? Can you describe these seizures for me?"

I opened and closed my mouth like a frightened fish, shocked, primarily, to be under the glare of the medical spotlight. Before I could reply, Dad butted in angrily.

"Shouldn't you be offering us some help instead of asking her stuff she can't answer?" he snapped. "Try answering my questions instead of asking more questions of your own!"

After an awkward silence, I was prescribed another slightly different form of medication and sent home.

"You make sure you take these new tablets every day," Dad told me. "I'll be checking up on you, Tricia. I know what you're like."

It suited Dad, of course, to keep me heavily medicated. Under the influence of Vigabatrin or Tegretol my memory was unreliable, and I was often sleepy, listless, and slightly vacant. Sitting in class, I was distracted, blinking away shoals of tiny floaters which swam across my eyeline and shimmery colours which crowded the sides of my vision. Sometimes, I felt as though I was hovering just on the edge of reality, and I couldn't quite find my way in.

Was I being locked out of the real world, on purpose, because nobody liked me? Or had I caused this myself, the same way I had caused the abuse from my father, and the seizures? Was this all my fault? Had I locked myself out?

If I had reported the sexual abuse by my father, at that age, I probably would not have been taken seriously and less still been believed. My account would likely have been dismissed as fantastical and unreliable, as the fictional product of my changing medication and an overactive child's imagination.

As part of the investigations into the increasing frequency of my seizures, I was booked in at the hospital for a couple of days of tests. On the day of my admission, everyone else left the house, for school and work, leaving just Dad and me at home. My legs felt leaden as I clambered out of bed and there was a molten dread in the base of my bowels which had nothing to do with the forthcoming trip to hospital.

"Tricia!" Dad shouted. "Get in here now. Get your pyjamas off."

He had no need even to keep his voice down. It made the whole disgusting ordeal seem weirdly mundane, as though this was as much a part of my morning chores as cleaning my teeth or feeding my guinea pigs before school. I was simply ticking off a task and nothing more.

At first, I was made to climb into the bed but then he ordered me to climb out and stand on the grubby pink carpet, bending over, facing away from him. My heart began to hammer. It was happening again. This was exactly how it had started in the living room. Any moment now, I'd feel the most horrendous, eviscerating pain and I would be cut clean into two.

"Keep still," Dad demanded.

But my knees would not stop shaking. Bunched up with nerves, I lifted my chin a little so that I could see the door, and sure enough, there she was on the landing; the lady with the lovely face. That was something, at least. Her presence meant so much to me.

"Please," I pleaded silently. "Please don't let him do it again. Stop him. Please."

Her face was illuminated with kindness, yet she was completely impotent; as helpless to stop him, as I was. The seconds dragged by, and it was like waiting for an axe to fall on my neck. My breathing was loud in my ears, as the seconds became minutes, yet there was no penetration and no pain. Then, Dad exhaled a satisfied, finalising breath, and said:

"Go and get dressed. We're going to be late for the hospital. Get a move on."

Again, so straightforward and deadpan, as though this was nothing out of the ordinary. He made it sound as though I had caused the delay and it was my fault we were running late. But I almost felt like singing out, throwing my arms around his girth, and thanking him. I was so grateful, so relieved, that it had not been worse. Quickly, before Dad changed his mind, I got myself dressed, had a quick breakfast, and then ran outside to feed my rabbits and hamsters in the shed.

"I'll be back soon," I promised, throwing extra pellets into the cages. I was worried they might be forgotten whilst I was away in hospital. Back in the house, I scooped some meat into the dogs' bowls and then I waited by the front door.

"Goodbye Tyson," I murmured, as he came to nuzzle my leg. "Stay out of his way, if you can."

Dad drove me to hospital in silence but the sheer proximity of him, in the driver's seat, made me flushed and fearful and a blotchy rash slithered out from my jumper and up the side of my face. I thought again of the assault in the bedroom, of the oppressive wait for the pain that never came. I was traumatised much more by what could have been, rather than by what I had actually endured.

At the hospital, Dad dropped me off, leaving after checking me in, without bothering to see me settled on the ward. I climbed into bed with my Baby Expressions tucked cosily under the blanket, by my side.

"You're safe now," I reminded myself. "Safe."

But panicky thoughts scuttled through my mind, like cockroaches. What if? What if? The searing pain of atrocity in the living room was as raw and as real now as it had been the moment it had happened. I had been so sure he was going to do it again that morning, that the sexual assault he had performed instead seemed almost inconsequential. All I could think of was the armchair, the stained glass in the living room door, the appalling, inhuman agony.

"Patricia?" asked a nurse. "Are you OK? You look a bit pale."

She was speaking to me from the bottom of a long and twisty tunnel. I watched in astonishment as her face stretched out and elongated as though it was made of chewing gum. I reached my hand out to hers, noticing her sparkly ring and bright nail polish, and then, everything went black. When I awoke, the same nurse was holding my hand.

"You're back with us," she smiled, smoothing my hair back from my face. "I think you had a little seizure there. How are you feeling?"

I had that familiar banging headache, as though there were gremlins shaking my brain, and I smiled weakly.

"I'm fine," I replied. "And thank you for asking."

She laid her hand on mine and I admired her blue nail polish. She asked me all about Baby Expressions and then she brought me a glass of cordial. That afternoon, I was sent for more scans and blood tests, and I was hooked up to a couple of different machines overnight.

The following day, with the doctors apparently happy with the results, I was allowed home again. Mum was at work and so Dad came to collect me. Again, with just me and him in

the car, the atmosphere was thick with fear, and I could prac-
tically taste it at the back of my throat.

I kept allowing myself sneaky glances at Dad's profile and I
noticed his teeth were set on edge. I watched the skin around
his jaw go pale and tight. And I knew there was trouble
ahead. When we arrived back home, Tyson bounded into
the hallway to greet me, offering me his one white paw as
a handshake, and Dad kicked him out of the way routinely.

"You've been sat in bed on your backside for two days," he
bellowed at me. "You can get this lot cleaned up for a start.
You lazy little shit."

He swept his arm around the kitchen, taking in the dirty
dishes, the morning's cereal boxes, the worksurfaces littered
with crumbs and sticky patches of strawberry jam.

"OK Dad," I said simply.

I settled my Baby Expressions down onto a dining chair
and set to work running a bowl of hot water and wiping
the surfaces. Dad stood and watched, bristling with a bitter
anger, itching to pull me up if I made a mistake.

He was irrationally furious, as though this whole mess,
permeating from the kitchen and spooling throughout our
entire lives, was all my doing. Ostensibly he was angry about
the kitchen, yet I felt his rage was linked somehow to the
abuse.

Looking back, I want to believe he loathed himself for
sexually abusing me, for the pain and anguish he caused
me. A naïve, hopeful part of me wants to believe he was
remorseful; conflicted and tormented. But the more realistic
voice inside my head argues he was probably just frightened

and furious for himself, and for the perilous position he had put himself in. And somewhere, in his warped mind, he had found a way to transfer that guilt and that hatred onto me. In his mind, he blamed me for being there, for being his victim. Clearly, I was the problem, and not him.

'It's not my fault, Tricia, remember that. Not my fault.'

10

"Hurry Up"

Following my seizure in the hospital bed, I had weekly follow-up appointments at the GP surgery. I didn't like seeing the doctor; all the attention brought me out in a cold, shivery sweat, and a re-emergence of the itchy red rash which crept like ivy from my chest, up my neck and onto my cheeks. And the closeness of my father, in the car, and in the appointment, side by side on plastic chairs, was menacing and unsettling for me.

I stared at his fingers, gripping the gear stick. I felt his coat sleeve, brushing against mine. I heard the low growl from his chest, and it was the same, slightly breathless sound, that he made in his bed. The fear was electrifying. One morning, we arrived for my regular check-up and the surgery car park was nearly full. Dad parked at the far side and as I got out of the car, he grabbed my hand in his.

"Stick with me, it's a busy car park," he said.

"Hurry Up"

Dad was not affectionate or tactile and generally the only purposeful physical contact between us was during the abuse.

"What do you care?" I wanted to yell. "Why would you bother if I was knocked down and killed? You hate me!"

But instead, I curled my small hand around his bigger one, and I smiled. In my heart, I wanted my hand in his; I yearned for that feeling of paternal protection and those assurances of safety and security. I wanted so much to believe that my father took my hand, because he wanted to look after me, because he loved me.

I was eight years old by now, but still just a little girl in desperate need of nurture. Yet the last time my father had taken my hand was in his bed, and he had forcibly guided me inside his shorts. Him holding my hand was a reminder of the depravity and the cruelty and the bare wickedness which festered in his heart. And in many ways, it was this which I feel damaged me irreparably; alongside the abuse, I was finding that all other simple pleasures, such as holding my father's hand, or sitting next to him, were tainted and infected. All physical contact with my father was associated with sexual abuse, with dread, and with doom.

The GP could find nothing wrong with me that day and even suggested reducing my medication, which irritated my father.

"She's had more fits, since that one in hospital," he said.

I didn't remember any at all.

"We're not even sure Patricia actually has epilepsy," the GP explained. "There might be another explanation for the seizures. And hopefully they might be temporary. Children do grow out of these things."

Dad glared at him, as if my improving health was an unwelcome set-back.

"I've made an application to the Family Fund at the hospital," he said. "I need a doctor to back me up. Can you do me a letter?"

The GP shook his head. That wasn't his department apparently. I squirmed on my seat, painfully aware that I was the cause of the trouble. I felt like a small bug, under a microscope, the light singeing my hair, a giant pair of tweezers gripping me around the neck.

Pop her on a slide with a drop of iodine and we'll have a proper look...

Dad continued arguing, and after a fruitless exchange, he left the surgery with me trailing warily in his wake. And in the car, the strain stretched out tightly, between us. I knew, ridiculous as it sounded, that Dad was irate with me for not being ill enough.

He drove on in angry silence, and I felt more and more apprehensive. I felt the sweat pooling, at the nape of my neck and trickling slowly down my back. Our drive home was along a quiet, leafy lane in Handforth, Cheshire, and without explanation, Dad suddenly pulled into a layby and switched off the engine.

He began unbuckling his belt. He was either going to thrash me with the belt, as he did the dogs, or he was going to make me do the unthinkable. My gut instinct told me it was the latter and I would so much rather have been beaten black and blue. He pulled his trousers down slightly and reached over to grab my hair, guiding my head downwards by force.

I didn't think about the chances of being spotted by passers-by. I didn't know what he was doing so I had no idea that it was wrong, criminal, perverted and debased beyond measure. Whether Dad got a particular kick out of abusing me in public, or whether he felt he simply could not wait until he got home, I would never know.

This attack in public was related, perhaps, to the way he left his bedroom door open, during the abuse, when there were people downstairs. It was another strand of his many perversions. I fixated on the smell. The foul, gagging, odious smell that stung the lining of my nose and made my eyes water. The smell I knew would follow me to my grave.

Just before Dad was finished, he pulled my head out of the way and ejaculated into a tissue. Again, the stench was rancid, filling the car like a toxic chemical bomb. Dad didn't seem to register either the odour or my distress. He simply restarted the car and drove home.

My eight-year-old's psyche did not know what to make of the incident, or how to cope with it. And so instead, I amputated the entire ordeal from my day and sealed it deep in the catacombs of my mind. And, like a typical child, with inbuilt self-preservation, I focussed on the things I understood.

The Spice Girls were storming the charts and Lisa and I were adoring fans. We practised our dance routines, after school and on every weekend. I had a pair of stretchy silver leggings and a grey top with frilly sleeves which I felt was the perfect outfit for Sporty Spice. She was my hero. I wore my hair in a high ponytail like hers and I copied all her moves. My favourite song was 'Wannabe' and I knew all the words off by heart.

'Yeah, I'll tell you what I want, what I really, really want
'So tell me what you want, what you really, really want'

When we weren't singing and dancing, we'd be jumping up and down the steps in the square or eating Rich Tea fingers in Lisa's kitchen.

"You can stay for your tea," Lisa's mum always said. "I'm doing pie and mash. Just make sure your dad doesn't mind."

"Oh, he won't mind," I replied. "I can promise you that."

Each afternoon, after school, I rushed home to look after my pets. I looked forward to shutting myself away in the dingy little shed and getting my rabbits and hamsters out of the cages for a cathartic cuddle. I loved feeling their noses snuffling into the palm of my hand, the rabbits' ears constantly twitching, always on the lookout for predators. Their vigilance reminded me of my own sixth sense.

"You're safe here Thumper," I murmured. "Safe with me."

I spent hour after hour in the dusty gloom of the tatty old shed, using the light from the kitchen windows to help me see as I cleared out the wet shavings and filled up the water bowls.

I loved how quiet and peaceful it was in there, in such contrast to the charged chaos of the house. The rabbits and hamsters made no noise at all. And when I spoke to them, it was in little more than a whisper:

"I'm going to Bluebell Woods with Tyson and Bonnie to find you some dandelions," I told them. "I'll bring them back for your supper."

The rabbits loved to have a hop around the shed whilst I cleaned the cages and it took me ages to catch them again, throwing myself headlong on the floor with my arms outstretched, cartoon-style. It was only me and them in the shed, but I'd find myself giggling out loud as they slipped through my fingers time after time. There was a feeling of shared fun and friendship and I felt so at home there, in the shed.

When my chores were done, I took Tyson and Bonnie out for walks around the estate. There was a grassy area which later became a skate-park, where I could let them off the leads for a run around. Often, on the lighter, warmer nights, I'd stop and sit on the wall for half an hour and read my favourite book. I'd learned my lesson, trying to read the packaging on food, and instead I'd become obsessed with the Goosebumps series. I could lose myself completely in the mystery world of ghosts and ghouls. Tyson and Bonnie were always happy to lie down and luxuriate in the early evening sunshine whilst I sounded out new words on the page:

'G-o-o-s-e-b-u-m-p-s – S-l-a-p-p-y w-o-r-l-d…'

Tyson was a handsome, black dog, with a white stripe down his chest and one white left paw. He had that comical way, whilst I was reading, of rocking from side to side, as though he was dancing. He knew it always made me laugh.

Those hours spent with my pets were an invaluable form of therapy for me. I arrived home with my pockets stuffed with clover and dandelion leaves for the rabbits and guinea pigs. There was just time to stuff the greens through their cages before I was shouted in for tea and bed. Strange as it might seem, I was a happy little girl, much of the time, content in my own, solitary world with my books and my animals for company, and the horrors of my other reality neatly packaged away.

* * * *

I was at yet another check-up at the hospital. Sitting on the chair, perfectly still and passive, trying to make myself as small and as unobtrusive as possible, I felt my hands and face becoming clammy. Even though I barely moved – I didn't even blink – the sweat and angst seemed to ooze as one out of every pore. I just couldn't help myself. I felt my old enemy, the red rash, crawling up my neck, and I blushed in embarrassment.

"Well, she's really been quite unwell," Dad was saying. "Still having the seizures. Tummy upsets. She's really struggling at school. Way behind all her targets."

It was a surprise to me. I wasn't top of the class and neither did I want to be. But I wasn't right at the bottom either. Considering I had so much time off sick, I was holding my own, hovering just below average levels.

At school, as at home, I got through my day without drawing attention to myself, doing what was asked of me and nothing more or less. And I wasn't aware of any seizures either, or any tummy upsets. I couldn't even remember the last time I'd had an epileptic fit. But I knew it was best to leave this sort of thing to my dad. If asked, I understood I was expected simply to parrot and confirm what he had already said. I wasn't exactly sure whether it was true, but I understood also that that wasn't really the most important issue.

"So, you'll consider referring us for the family fund?" Dad asked, as he got to his feet. "At least review it?"

"No. Not at the moment, Mr King," replied the doctor.

My school shirt was sticking to my chest as I followed Dad out of the surgery. I couldn't work out why I was so sweaty, and why I had such a prescient feeling of doom. I hadn't seen my face, but I could tell I was covered in raised red blotches. And as if to complete my humiliation, Dad sneered:

"Let yourself down again Tricia, with that stupid rash. You look a right mess. Pull yourself together."

After the appointment, the plan was for Dad to drop me back at school, it was only mid-morning. Instead, he drove towards home. By now, my anxiety was escalating into panic and warning signals were screaming inside my head.

"No, please, not today."

The words scudded through my mind, but I said nothing. We reached the same, leafy lane where it had happened before. As Dad indicated and pulled in, at the exact same spot, I began trembling. He undid his trousers and nodded at me.

"Hurry up," he muttered. "Not much time. You need to get to your lessons."

It baffled me how on the one hand, he was a father who was apparently anxious about me missing my education and falling behind at school. Yet he was also a hideous and hateful beast. There was no crossover, no middle ground between the two. Again, it was the smell which stuck with me, which haunted me, and which would live with me for the rest of my life.

11

Summer Holiday

That summer, Dad announced he and his brother would be taking me and my cousin on holiday to Spain.

"Spain!" I gasped. "Wow! Just wow!"

I was lost for words. I had never been on holiday. I'd never even been to Rhyl or Prestatyn or Scarborough, never mind anywhere as exotic as Spain. The announcement was as shocking as it was exciting.

We flew from Manchester Airport, which was in itself a thrill, later landing in Malaga. We stayed in an apartment, Dad and his brother in one room, me and my cousin in another. The apartments were attached to a hotel complex and so we had full use of the pool and the hotel's entertainment.

I had learned to swim by now, and though I still harboured a fear of water, I wanted to cool off and splash around with all the other children. But I was horrified by the big bugs I'd spotted floating on the surface of the water and was worried they might bite me.

"Oh, just jump in, Tricia," scoffed my dad, as he threw his towel on a sunbed and dived in. "Stop being such a whiner. It's one thing after another with you, you're never satisfied."

It was typical of me, I knew, to replace my swimming phobia with a bug phobia. My neuroses seemed to stretch endlessly; one waiting to usurp the next. I was a nervous, worried, jittery little girl and my father's ridicule just made me all the more uneasy. I didn't realise then, chewing my lip at the edge of the water, that my father was responsible for my anxieties. Yet here he was mocking me about them. Just as he was responsible for my epilepsy, yet he was in charge of my medical appointments.

It was a cruel irony and one which he was probably very smug about. It felt like he had it all wrapped up; like he was conducting every instrument in the orchestra and I was just the little triangle, hunched in the percussion corner, waiting for his permission to hit a note. And so, I spent most of my time in Spain sitting on the poolside, dangling my legs in the water and keeping a close eye on the wildlife, whilst my back and shoulders burned pinkish red in the sun.

At night, I was mesmerised by the hotel's dancers, who wore exotic outfits, heavy eye make-up and glamorous red lipstick. One of the dancers seemed to smile directly at me, every night, and I smiled back broadly. I really felt as though I had made a new friend, even though we had never even spoken.

Away from his jibes about the water, Dad mostly left me

alone that week. He was busy drinking with my uncle and ogling the women in the outside bar areas. His favourite chat up line for strangers was to tell them about his role as a swimming coach and he organised races in the pool for some of the children, to impress their mothers. Left to our own devices, my cousin and I had a wonderful time. I used all my pesetas to buy a small Gizmo teddy with rubber ears, identical to my own, as a gift for Lisa.

On the journey home, I ate so many Maltesers I was almost sick on the aeroplane and stepping out onto the grey tarmac at 5am and into the Manchester drizzle brought with it its own type of sickness. I did not want to go home again, and to everything it represented.

After just a few days back in Wilmslow, back to the arguing, the over-crowding, the sexual abuse, it was as though my trip to Spain was nothing more than a fanciful dream; a product of my medication or my imagination. The only proof it had been real was Lisa's Gizmo, which sat on her pillow.

The trip was a complete anomaly in my childhood, totally unlike anything which had gone before it or which followed. Only later, I would look back, and wonder whether the Spanish holiday, like the Baby Expressions, was a bribe. A hush-holiday. A glittering incentive for me to keep my mouth tightly shut.

* * * *

By now, there was a very clear link in my mind between Dad offering me chocolate and treats, and then abusing me. And yet, each time it happened, I could not help kidding myself, just a little bit, convincing myself that this time, unlike any other time, his motives might be different.

The bigger part of me wanted so much to believe I had a father, a daddy, like other children, who wanted to share his chocolates with me, and nothing more besides. I longed to be able to sit next to him, on the sofa, and bicker over a bag of chocolate buttons whilst we watched Saturday night telly, without worrying about what was expected of me in return.

"Here Tricia," he called, spotting me sidling past the living room door. "Bag of chocolate raisins here. Hold your hand out."

I wanted to offer him my hand and yet I wanted to snatch it away. As Dad poured a few raisins into my palm, I heard one of my brothers grumbling under his breath in the kitchen.

'You have no idea what I have to do in exchange for eight chocolate raisins,' I said silently, solemnly. 'No idea at all.'

I would have done without chocolates for the rest of my life if it meant an end to the morning abuse. But it didn't work like that. In my thoughts, the sweets played a pivotal part in making me feel responsible, as though I was somehow to blame for the abuse. I'd accepted them, after all, without question. And so perhaps I deserved what was coming. Each time I accepted a sweet, it was a small pick me up, a kernel of hope that perhaps his intentions were genuine. Maybe this was the start of him becoming a proper father. But the following morning, every time, my hopes were smashed to pieces, and I was left feeling guilty and ashamed and despairing.

I was knocked down, like a little wooden skittle, and it got harder and harder to pick myself up again. And of course, there were times I was horribly abused without bribe or reward. Which was worse?

I have no idea what Dad's thought processes were. I don't know in what bizarre and perverted world he lived, where it was OK to sexually abuse your own daughter in exchange for a couple of squares of Bourneville chocolate. And I would never know, because I would never dare challenge him. Just as my brother would never dare voice his frustration that he never got chocolates, as I did. Just as I could never find the courage within me to one morning run past his bedroom door and ignore his warped demands. I imagined it often enough: Dad calling my name and me shouting:

"No! I'm not doing it! I don't want to come into the bedroom. I don't want any chocolates. I'm not going for any more hospital appointments. I'm not taking the medicine! Leave me alone!"

I pictured myself stalking down the stairs with my ghostly friend looking on in silent slack-jawed admiration. I got to the door, I took Tyson's lead from the kitchen counter, and off we went on our adventures.

It was a sunny day, we had a picnic, and we were headed for Bluebell Woods. I loved the daydream. But of course that's all it was and all it ever would be. Yet, my continuing passivity and compliance seemed to make Dad more and more arrogant and cavalier. He regularly kept me home from school, sometimes with a half-baked excuse about my health, other times he didn't seem even to bother with the pretence.

He watched pornography on the family TV downstairs, calling me to him at whatever point he felt the urge. He knew my mother and my siblings could come home at any time and catch him abusing me. He knew I could report him. Yet he was as supreme as he was evil. He was completely untouchable.

In years to come, I would blame myself, realising that speaking out might have been the very thing needed to break the cycle. But I didn't have the words. I didn't have the courage. I had worked so hard at going unnoticed that now I had shrunk right back inside myself; I was impenetrable, unreachable, even to myself. I could not speak out, not then. Yet whatever I did, it would have been wrong. I was brought up and reminded every day that it was all my fault. And I'd have blamed myself, no matter how it ended, because I was brainwashed to do so.

12

Garden Of Death

At the end of September 1996, we went for our annual trip to Blackpool Illuminations and by the time we got home, it was late. Climbing into my bunk, I heard an unusual scrabbling sound coming from the Guinea pig tank by the window, but knew I'd get into trouble if I put the light on to investigate. Early the next morning, I was woken by my two Guinea pigs, Snowy and Toffee, squeaking and whistling, and when I looked into the tank, I gasped in amazement.

"Babies!" I exclaimed in excitement. "Well done!"

There were three tiny little balls of light brown fur inside of the tank, curled up and still with their eyes tightly closed. I christened them Baby-toffee, Choccy and Pip. I made my announcement at breakfast and my older siblings decided we should move the animals outside to the shed immediately, and into separate cages, so the male was no longer with the female and her babies.

I spent the day happily making a new home for them, filling the cages with soft sawdust, before carrying the little family down from my bedroom.

"There," I said proudly, as they settled into their new cages. "You'll be warm and cosy here."

There was a wooden block in the shed, and I used it as a little stool, whilst I took out each hamster and rabbit in turn for a cuddle. I knew Snowy needed time with her babies and so I left her alone for a few days. There was a padlock on the shed, and I triple checked each night that it was locked, to keep her and her babies safe.

In the mornings before school, and every afternoon when I got home, I dashed to the shed to check on them, first grabbing the padlock key from the kitchen worktop, and always making sure it was replaced. When the babies got a little older, I began taking them out of the cage, one by one, for cuddles. I adored them all.

"Just you wait until the summer, and we can make a run for you in the garden," I told them. "You can have races with the rabbits, and I'll bring you clover for your breakfast."

One morning, Mum was uncharacteristically off work unwell, which in turn meant I had a temporary reprieve from my father's abuse. I had noticed his fuse was even shorter than usual recently; he seemed grumpy and raring to argue and fight with everyone he came across.

I'd been very careful to tiptoe past him, head down, almost believing that if I couldn't see him, he couldn't see me either. I tried to keep Tyson and Bonnie away from his eye-line too. My main aim of today, as each day, was to stay below the visibility line, and somehow go unnoticed and unpunished. Scampering downstairs, I felt a ripple of excitement at the prospect of seeing the three babies and giving them a customary cuddle before school.

It was portentously gloomy outside, a dull, drizzly Autumn morning and the light was poor, casting a slightly ghoulish shadow across the garden. Taking the padlock key, I let myself out of the back door, and opened the shed. There was just enough light from the kitchen window for me to make out the shapes of the cages and the animals. Once inside, I opened the babies' cage and picked up the one nearest.

Instantly, I knew something was wrong.

Glancing down, I saw tufts of fur and skin, and the glassy eyes of a dead animal. The little body was in pieces. There was a flaking, breaking, feeling inside my chest, as though my insides were falling away. As though I, too, was falling apart. It took a few seconds for my brain to catch up with what my eyes were seeing, and then, in horror, I dropped the corpse back into the cage and fled into the house, screaming. Mum came hurtling down the stairs in her nightie.

"Whatever's happened?" she asked.

"The baby is dead! Baby-toffee is dead!" I sobbed hysterically. "Come and see! My poor Guinea pigs."

Mum went out to the shed and when she returned, she said to me:

"You can't go into school in that state. I'll call your teacher and let her know."

I spent most of the morning crying under my duvet, unable to shake the memory of the little body in my hand.

"Poor Baby-Toffee," I wept.

That night, around the dinner table, my older siblings discussed the death, not in the respectful way I would have hoped, but more as a fascinating who-dunnit.

"Someone killed it," said one of my brothers. "Definitely. It was sliced right through. Whoever did that meant business alright."

I felt my heart splintering. Despite the state of the Baby-toffee's little body, it had not occurred to me that this was a deliberate act. I had presumed it was some sort of dreadful illness. I couldn't believe anyone could be so cruel.

"Who would do that?" replied another brother. "Gross."

My father chewed through his lamp chop and said nothing.

* * * *

On my way out of school assembly the next morning, the deputy-head nodded at me and pulled me aside. She was a tall, too thin, woman with very short grey hair, cut into a severe, no-nonsense style.

"And where were you yesterday, Patricia King?" she demanded, her cold blue eyes drilling through mine.

She was very well-spoken and often corrected the children, and even the other teachers, on our Northern pronunciations.

"My baby guinea pig died," I replied, shuddering at a flashback of the body parts. "Baby-Toffee."

She sighed, as if I had disappointed her greatly.

"The death of a pet is not a good reason to have a day off

school," she said. "You have so much time off as it is. Don't let it happen again. Do you understand?"

I nodded and hurried off to class with tears pricking my eyes. I hated being singled out, and I was not used to being told off at school. I was mortified. Yet her lack of sympathy bothered me even more.

That afternoon, after I finished my lessons, I went straight to the shed to feed my pets. The remains of the baby had been cleared away, and the other two babies, their parents, and the rabbits and hamsters, all seemed perfectly fine. I dismissed the conversation around the dinner table and convinced myself it was a one-off tragedy, a random illness, maybe a virus, which had claimed just one life. I could not explain why the tiny body was in pieces – and such precise pieces too – and so I pushed that to the back of my consciousness.

"You're all OK," I told my pets, as I padlocked the door, with far more authority than I felt.

The following morning, I was a little apprehensive as I grabbed the padlock key and made my way outside. The morning was grey again and it was as though the weather itself was feeling mournful and depressed, mirroring my own distress. I opened the cage, cautiously - and shrieked. There, in exactly the same spot as his brother, was a second dead baby. This time, it was dear little Choccy. Again, the tiny body seemed to have been dissected. Yelling and stumbling out of the shed, I dashed into the house.

"Oh, not again," sighed one of my brothers. "This is really weird."

I did not dare take another day off school, and so, trembling, I splashed my face with cold water and had a drink of milk. I couldn't face any breakfast.

Much as I was terrified of going back to the shed, I knew I couldn't leave the animals without food. It took a superhuman bravery for me to go back outside, to feed and reassure them. Now, as last time, the little corpse had vanished. It was as though poor Choccy had never existed. Pip, the remaining baby guinea pig, stared at me from a lonely corner of the cage, and I felt an odd rush of sympathy and terror for him. Would he be next?

* * * *

I was a bundle of nerves as I made my way outside the following morning. I could almost have been predicting a seizure, my senses felt hyper-alert, my heartbeat was fast and frenzied. But this time, all I perceived was pure fear.

It was darker still today, there were clouds like purple bruises hanging ominously low in the sky, and I shivered involuntarily. As the back door swung open into the darkness of the garden, I suddenly caught sight of a face, pale and ghostly, in the glass panel, and I screamed out loud. In the next moment, I realised the face was my own, simply my reflection in the glass.

"Stop it, Trish," I told myself crossly. "Get a grip."

But my heart was still pounding. My teeth chattered as I unlocked the padlock, on tiptoe, and crept inside the shed, relying as usual on the faint kitchen light to illuminate the cages. There was a scurrying sound which normally would bring me comfort; a sign my pets were saying hello. But now the noise panicked and frightened me. Were they running towards me, or were they running away? And from what?

Peering into the babies' cage, I let out a howl. There, lying motionless, was poor Pip. Gagging, I reached out one finger towards him, but I knew it was hopeless. I knew, by now, what dead bodies looked like. He was stiff and cold.

"Bye baby Pip," I sobbed.

That night, around the dining table, we had relatives visiting, and I felt as though they and my older siblings chatted about the death of my baby guinea pigs as though it was an item of neighbourhood gossip. Inwardly, I felt revolted and outraged by the lack of reverence, but I pushed my food around my plate and remained silent.

"The shed is locked every night and still locked each morning," my brother pointed out. "So our killer obviously has a key."

"Could it not be some sort of illness? Or a fight between the other guinea pigs?" asked one of the others.

"Course not," someone else replied. "Work it out. The last baby died in a cage all on its own. Anyway, they're all sliced into strips. There's something weird going on."

My stomach was roiling. I couldn't bear to hear my precious pets discussed with such little respect. The image of their bodies in neat strips was graphic in my mind, and I saw a ghastly picture of a big pair of hands holding Baby-Toffee still on a chopping board, his eyes wide with panic as he was sliced up like a loaf of bread. Just then my father, who had been out at work, put his key in the front door, and the entire table fell silent.

"What?" my father growled, scanning our faces. "What now?"

Nobody spoke. Nobody dared. But I could not shake the vision of my poor pet, on a chopping board, the knife hovering over his head. A couple of days passed without any further fatalities, and I tried to convince myself it was over. Whatever malevolent and murderous presence had visited our house, had now moved on.

Early on the third morning, as I got out of bed, Dad's bedroom door was ominously, agonisingly, ajar, and he called my name as I made my way past.

"In here, Tricia!" he shouted.

Swallowing down my revulsion, I climbed into his bed and did as I was told, peering out onto the landing for the ghost lady with her compassionate smile. I loved her long skirts, with all the ruffles. I wondered if I'd ever have a skirt like that. I liked her hair too; tumbling curls piled high on her head. I was learning to detach myself so completely from the abuse and force myself to instead concentrate on the trivial and inconsequential details around me. It was my way of surviving. Dad's bedroom was like a timeless void, where I was sucked into a terrifying vortex, whilst the rest of the household, and the outside world, moved on oblivious and unconcerned.

"Remember," Dad said to me, with the usual tremor in his voice. "This isn't my fault. I was made this way. You know I am scared of prison."

When it was over, I pulled my pyjamas back on and ran downstairs, in my slippers, to check on my pets in the shed outside. My mind still clouded by the sexual abuse, and the vision of my ghostly friend, I did not think too clearly about what I might find.

I opened the cage door where Snowy, the mother guinea pig lived, I knew, instantly, she was dead. In the adjacent cage, Toffee, the father guinea pig, was immobile and cold also.

"No," I gasped, clamping my hand over my mouth. "Please, no."

It was horrible. After three days without any deaths, I had been lulled into a false sense of security. And now this. Two at once, and both my lovely guinea pigs. It was too barbaric, gruesome and twisted to comprehend. I could not bear to stay in the shed a moment longer. I ran, wailing, into the garden. Inconsolable, I sat on the back step and sobbed, and felt Tyson's warm breath on my neck.

"Snowy and Toffee are dead," I told him solemnly. "Murdered."

At school, their mutilated bodies were all I could think of. Yet remembering how annoyed the teacher had been, after I told her about the death of Baby-Toffee, I felt it best to keep these more recent tragedies to myself. Ironically, these latest casualties would doubtless have sparked alarm amongst my teachers. Five deaths were so much more suspicious than one. But I had been put firmly in my place by the deputy-head, and I didn't trust anyone enough to confide in them about my home-life. And neither did I want to make a fuss.

That night, in bed, my mind ran wild with possibilities. Where would this end? What if the murderer came back for Tyson and Bonnie? What if they came for me?

Fear clutched at my heart like an icy hand. If my pets were not safe in a padlocked shed, what chance did I have in a broken bunkbed with only my Baby Expressions and my Gizmo teddy on my side? I could not sleep, instead freezing at every creaking floorboard, every noisy bed spring, every muffled groan. What if the bogeyman had sneaked his way into our house and he was on his way upstairs, to get me?

Or - what if he had been here all along?

The next day, I had to force myself to go out to the shed. Only the thought of my rabbits and hamsters starving to death propelled me out, through the back door, as if on auto-pilot. My legs didn't feel like my own and I was so afraid.

There was a familiar, reassuring thump coming from one cage. But in the cage where two of the rabbits, Floppy and Thumper, lived together, there was silence. Seeing their bodies, much bigger and more substantial than the guinea pigs, was sickening. Floppy looked intact on the surface and so, rigid with fear, I prodded him a little, only to scream out in terror when underneath he was neatly sliced and dissected. It was a ghastly trick. My own insides swirled and curdled as I looked at Floppy's internal organs, spilling out into the cage.

"Help!" I yelled, in a thin, frightened voice. "Somebody please help me!"

Nobody came and, with my eyes almost closed, I managed to throw some food into the cages for Popsy, my remaining rabbit, and the two hamsters. By the time I got outside, into the fresh air, I was retching and shuddering so violently that it took me several attempts to close the padlock.

"Floppy and Thumper," I told Tyson sadly. "Gone."

I could have sworn his eyes were shiny with tears. He was the only one who truly understood. Once again, as with all the other animals, the rabbits' bodies disappeared quickly and efficiently.

The whole episode was as baffling as it was sinister. I had no idea what was going on, or when it was going to end. That same week, I found Po, my little grey and white hamster dead. The next day, my second hamster, Lala, was also dead. Both were dismembered, just like the others. Both cold, stiff, and with unseeing eyes.

The row of empty cages was heart-breaking; a physical reminder of what I had lost and how much they had suffered. With both my little hamsters gone, that now left only my remaining rabbit, Popsy.

"Promise you won't leave me too," I whispered, sitting on the wooden block and holding her face close to mine. Like her siblings, she was mainly white with spots of black, grey and orange. I could feel her body quivering, under her fur. Like me, she could sense the fear. She could taste the danger. She knew what was ahead. The following morning, she, too, was dead.

* * * *

There was a thin thread of relief, running through the shock and grief, that it was, at least, all over. Every day, for weeks,

I had woken with a sickness in the pit of my stomach, worrying over which of my beloved pets would be next to the slaughter. Now my animals were dead, there were no more questions, there was no more uncertainty. Ten needless, brutal deaths. Ten loving, innocent animals. I missed them so much.

"I'm sorry," I sobbed. "I'm sorry I couldn't protect you."

I was used to being blamed for everything and I took responsibility for this too.

Tyson and Bonnie remained, but even as a little girl, I knew they were safe. I sensed they wouldn't be so easily diced and sliced, as my rabbits, hamsters and guinea pigs had been. My dogs, I recognised, would fight back. Whoever had killed the other pets was a bully and on that basis I reckoned they would not target my dogs. But poor Popsy and Choccy and Thumper had been helpless and afraid and had probably died with little fuss and little fight, but in lots of pain. I thought of myself, a frightened little rabbit, passively going into Dad's bedroom, time after time, helpless, afraid, and in a great deal of pain.

My ninth birthday passed by in a blur. All I could think of were the broken little bodies of my furry friends, thrown into the bin or even just tossed down the garden to rot. I had no idea what had happened to their remains and I was tormented by images of them decaying in the undergrowth. Memories of their unseeing eyes loomed in my dreams. Bursts of fear, deadly reminders, like a killer shark's fin, shot through my mind. Sometimes I woke, sweating and disorientated, shouting their names:

"Snowy! Toffee! Po!"

"You had another seizure in the night," Dad said, the next morning. "You need to take more medication. I'll mention it to the doctor. You're staying off school today."

I shrugged helplessly. There was a dull ache of sadness, deep inside me, which no medication would ever cure. The horror of the deaths was all too quickly forgotten in the house. My pets became another subject which we just didn't mention, without really knowing why.

13

He's Gone

Not long after Popsy's death, I was woken one night by a big argument raging downstairs. I was used to rows, but this one, between my parents, sounded much worse than usual. Creeping along the landing, I made my way downstairs, taking care to avoid the carpet tacking on the bare stairs where I had blacked out and fallen during my worst seizure.

Dad was on his usual sofa in the living room, Mum was in the kitchen, and they were screaming at each other. There was a brief pause in the shouting, followed by a loud smash. I hurried along the hallway to peep around the living room door and see what was going on. On our telly, we had a big, ugly clock with eagle wings sprouting from the sides. It had been a fixture in our home right through my childhood, but now, it lay smashed into pieces on the carpet. Moments later, the front door slammed, and Dad was gone.

In that moment, my heightened sensitivity detected a calm

descending upon the house, almost a sort of cleansing. It felt like a bloated toxic cloud had been squeezed out through the window and dissolved into the night air.

He had gone.

Soon after, my older siblings, along with more relatives, arrived at the house, and the discussion and argument began again. Everyone had a point of view, each louder and more forceful than the last. I crept back up the stairs to the halfway turn and huddled at the side, with my nightie pulled over my knees to keep me warm, and my Baby Expressions in my arms. The sniping ran back and forth like gunfire.

"It's disgusting," one was saying. "And against a child. How could he?"

"We don't know if it's true," said another voice. "It's just an allegation. He hasn't been charged yet."

"Give me strength!" snorted another. "Course he did it."

Something in the conversation tugged at the back of my mind; a link I was trying to make but wasn't quite able to stretch the two strands to meet in the middle.

"You don't know that," said the second voice again. "You can't accuse someone of child abuse without knowing for certain."

"I do!" retorted the first voice. "He's a paedophile. A bloody paedophile."

In that moment, the link snapped into place, like a headlamp switching onto full beam. My whole mind was lit up, with a white light. A peculiar feeling gripped me; it was a little bit like the moments before a seizure; a dawning, a real-isation, a mind-blowing epiphany. I took Baby Expressions tightly in my arms and whispered, "He did do it. I know he did. Because he did it to me too."

* * * *

Morning came, and there was still no sign of my father. For a few days, nothing much was different. The house was as noisy and disorganised as ever and I had yet another outbreak of head lice which was causing me great discomfort and embarrassment.

We eventually ran out of milk. I shrugged and poured dry rice crispies for my breakfast, disappointed by the lack of crackle, which was one of my favourite parts of my morning routine. It wasn't ideal, but I didn't dwell on it. We ran out of dog food too and I began feeding Tyson and Bonnie with scraps from the fridge. Normally, I'd have had my legs slapped for helping myself from the fridge but there didn't seem to be anyone around to tell me off.

"Here Tyson, here Bonnie," I said, throwing them both a sausage.

Tyson did his funny little dance, rocking back and forth on his legs. I opened the window so that he could dive in and out and make me laugh. I amused myself like that for hours, playing with the dogs, and suiting myself.

Weekend came and went, and Mum wasn't around either. I presumed she was working a double shift. It was exhilarating, being able to play out all weekend, with the kids from the estate. There was nobody to order me about or to make me do my chores.

"You must promise to be in for dark," said my older brother.

That seemed to be the only rule and I was happy with it. And even after bedtime, I stayed up late, reading in bed, with Tyson lying on my feet all night. I felt wonderfully free and untethered; for the first time, I could actually breathe.

One morning, I glanced at my epilepsy medication, piled high on a shelf under the archway to the kitchen, and realised there was nobody here to make sure I took it. Nobody at all. I was not a rule breaker and yet I felt a sudden surge of rebellion.

"What do you think, Tyson?" I asked, showing him the tablets.

He sniffed encouragingly, and it was all the back-up I needed. I was not devious enough to flush the pills down the loo or throw them away, I just left the packets untouched. At first, the empowerment was dizzying. I loved it. I was doing exactly as I liked. But even then, underneath the fizz of excitement, there was a sinister feeling of worry and inevitability. I sensed that this wild adventure could not last.

Sure enough, the days passed and, still with no sign of my father, the household toppled slowly, inevitably, into an even deeper level of chaos than we were already used to. We had no clean towels in the bathroom and the empty loo rolls formed a small mountain by the side of the sink. The bins overflowed, and the bills piled up, unopened, unnoticed, behind the front door. My eldest sibling still living at home was just a teenager himself, and though he did his best, I was not his responsibility.

"Make sure you're in by dark," was all he could think of by way of parental guidance.

Early one Monday morning, I made myself late for school as I searched the clean laundry for my school uniform, eventually finding it in the dirty washing pile, where I had left it on Friday afternoon.

"What am I going to do, Tyson?" I asked him and he stared at me, unblinking.

I had no choice but to put on the grubby uniform and smooth out the creases. I found a deodorant in the bathroom and gave myself a liberal spray. It was a male, woody scent, but better than sweat. That night, I worked out how to use the washing machine and Tyson and I watched the uniform whirring round, mesmerizingly, before hanging it up to dry. I tidied the kitchen too, washing dishes and mopping the floor. I was fast realising the downside of me stopping my chores was that nobody else did them either. I didn't want to live with rules. But then I didn't want to live in a hovel either.

"Just us here for tea," I told the dogs, as I defrosted a bag of meatballs. "I'll share with you both."

It was quite cosy, our picnic supper, on the kitchen floor, and certainly more peaceful than our usual family mealtimes. Afterwards, I washed and dried our dishes and found a cloth to scrub the worktops. I surveyed the tidy kitchen with warm approval. This was a little like having my own dolls' house.

"All done," I smiled happily.

Mum was working overtime, but she reappeared every few days, bringing with her bags of food shopping, or sometimes money for us to do a shop for ourselves, before vanishing again, for another double shift at work. There was no routine whatsoever.

I was used to disorder and mess, but this was spiralling to another level completely. Our lives became uncertain and unpredictable, lunging from one crisis to another, like poor penguins, leaping between melting ice caps. One day, we were sure to plunge into the icy waters and drown. Some mornings, there was no cereal. Other times, I had no clean underwear. I was solely responsible for taking my epilepsy medication, mornings and evenings, and, after that first buzz of insurrection, I had dutifully started to take it again. But sometimes, mistakenly, I forgot about it. Occasionally, I worried I might have taken it twice. The side-effects continued to drag me down, and, since my father was no longer around, I missed several hospital check-ups.

I decided to write a letter, to my consultant, to ask if my medication could be changed or even stopped completely. I had read a news article about a man who managed his epilepsy purely through his diet, and I wondered if I could try that too.

'When I wake up…' I wrote, 'my legs feel as if they are still asleep. I often get very uncomforting back pains…I think all of these problems are side effects of the tablets..'

I posted the letter and hoped for the best. In the meantime, as the weeks went by, I became less and less comfortable with the domestic turbulence at our house. Like any child, I longed for reassurance and structure, I needed rules and I wanted someone to take the reins. Yet the only constant in my life seemed to be my two dogs, and my Baby Expressions.

I felt so lonely. Even my ghost lady had vanished, as mysteriously and abruptly as she had first appeared. I hadn't seen her at all since that last incident of sexual abuse from my father. I longed to see her, I had so much to tell her. I even perched on the landing, staring at her usual spot, hoping she might suddenly shimmer into existence.

"Please," I pleaded silently. "You don't need to talk to me. I just want to see your face. Please."

But there was nothing.

One day, whilst I was at school, my period came. I'd heard a couple of my friends announcing their first period with real excitement and pride. But for me, there was no coming of age; no sensation of celebration, to mark the beginning of puberty. I felt my period was linked, inexplicably and malevolently, with the sexual abuse. It was something to be ashamed of, not heralded.

In the same way that I had never been able to bring myself to change the nappies for Baby Expressions, I now could not see the start of my periods as in any way the beginnings of a bright new chapter. All afternoon, I carried my secret around with me, doing my best to keep myself clean with frequent visits to the toilets. But that night, in bed, I began bleeding more heavily and realised I could no longer keep this to myself. I knew I'd be in real trouble if I stained the sheets.

My mother was home after a day shift and tentatively, I knocked on her bedroom door. It had been permanently closed since my father left, which I found at once disturbing and comforting. It was reassuring to know he wasn't in there, waiting to call my name. Yet the tightly closed door now seemed unfriendly and so very final.

"Come in," my mother called.

Swallowing back my tears, I found it difficult, just to form the words to tell her my news, and afterwards, she said:

"There are sanitary towels in your sister's room. Take a packet for yourself."

My first bra, which I began wearing soon after, was a hand-me-down from my big sister too. I was an early developer and, for once, I was the envy of the other girls in my class when they spotted my bra straps through my school shirt. But the clamour of attention around me was a bit like the unsightly rash creeping up my neck. I felt like a small animal at the zoo, an exhibit, under a spotlight, being poked and prodded by a string of visitors. *See if she bites when you hit her with this stick! Does she change colour?* Does she eat worms? I didn't want to stand out nor did I want to answer any questions. I certainly didn't want a bra, I didn't want to become a young woman, I didn't want to be attractive to boys. I didn't want to be attractive to anyone at all.

* * * *

When the weekend came, Mum went off to work again, and I was plunged into another state of limbo. No sooner was she back, than she'd disappear off for another shift, and I had no warning or idea of when she might return. It was like having frequent power cuts, pitching my life into turmoil and dark-ness, without any idea how long each one might last.

Week after week, the situation continued, always with a sense that something would have to give. I walked to school each morning with a scrunched-up ball of anxiety in my chest, knowing this off-grid, anarchic living would one day implode, yet not knowing how to prevent it.

It never occurred to me, once, to confide in a teacher or another adult that my father had vanished, and my mother was working away. I would never willingly have put myself under scrutiny. I didn't even confide in any school friends, probably through shame or a desire just to fit in and be the same as they were. Looking back, there were a couple of sets of parents who clearly realised something was wrong, who did their best to help by feeding me and inviting me to sleep over. One morning, a teacher noticed a mark on my knee and asked me:

"Is that a cigarette burn on your leg, Patricia?"

I shook my head. I explained it was a burn from a hot chocolate, caused by our dining table collapsing at the wrong moment, and she didn't question me further. I didn't realise it then, but it was an odd question to ask a young child and she must have been concerned about me. Yet she didn't raise it again. She gave me no indication that she worried about me more than my classmates, or that I was any different in any way from them, apart from my dreaded head lice.

One week, we had a sex education class, which caused general hilarity and embarrassment amongst my peers. But I felt horribly uneasy. As with the onset of puberty and my misgivings over Baby Expressions' nappy changing, I felt this was connected to my father.

"It's important to understand that sexual contact must always be between consenting adults. Now, let's talk about what we think that means…"

Whilst an animated discussion went around me, I felt like I was sinking – down, through my chair, through the classroom floor, into a dark and endless void. The teacher's words confirmed what I had suspected since my father was arrested. I was not an adult. I was not consenting. The sexual abuse was wrong, wrong, wrong.

"Patricia?" said the teacher. "Are you with us?"

She stared straight at me, her eyes boring through me, and I wondered why she was addressing me directly. Did she know? Did she suspect? And if she did know, why wasn't she trying to help? Perhaps, I told myself, she, too, thought it was my fault.

"Yes," I managed eventually. "I'm listening, Miss."

I half-expected to be kept back, after class, and grilled. But I was allowed to file out, with everyone else. There was no special treatment.

So I wasn't sure my teachers would even be interested in my home life, less still able to intervene and help me. Even if I had wanted to share my burden, I was still smarting from the deputy-head teacher's indifferent reaction to Baby-Toffee's death and I was not about to lay myself open to be curtly dismissed once again.

I didn't think my current situation was any worse than the one before. In many ways, it was far preferable. With my father out of the way, the abuse had stopped as abruptly as it had begun. There was no fanfare, no line in the sand, no big announcement. He sexually abused me one morning and the next morning, he did not. I didn't know then, and for many months to come, that it was over. The end of the abuse came as more of a creeping realisation, a gradual awareness that I was free. Bizarrely though, as the weeks went by, the sexual abuse, associated with my father's disappearance, was not uppermost in my mind. More than anything, I missed my dad. He was a bad-tempered, cruel bully. He was a twisted, evil, paedophile. Yet he was also my father. He gave structure to my life, he took me for days out, he cooked sausage and chips for my tea. If I couldn't find my school shoes, or I couldn't do my homework, I could ask my father for help. He wouldn't often give it, but he was always there to be asked. He was a constant; like school, like rain, like early bedtimes. I didn't necessarily like these things. But equally, I would be lost without them. And so, my first thought, when my father was no longer there, was not how grateful I was, but more how I wished he would come home.

When the sexual abuse stopped, my seizures were simultaneously miraculously cured, something which seemed an amazing coincidence to me at the time, but now the correlation seems perfectly logical. And in addition to the lack of fits, I had no father there to record them, or fabricate records of them. So from dominating my daily life for so long, they now became a condition which I thought of only in relation to the side-effects of the medication. When Mum was not working, she made sure I was keeping up with my tablets, which produced the same, numbing, draining side-effects. I had standard hospital check-ups, far less frequent than before, because my father was not around to demand extra appointments and extra medication. Also, I missed several appointments.

Nobody even opened the hospital letters. They stacked up in the hallway with the rest of the mail, which I didn't mind at all. It was only as the weeks rolled into months that I slowly began daring to appreciate the freedom of running past my father's bedroom door, in the morning, without fear of him calling out my name. There was nobody to force me to stay off school, nobody to raise my feeble hopes with offers of chocolate or fizzy drinks, nobody to destroy me physically and emotionally.

It should have been a big relief that my father was gone, and it was. But there was an overwhelming sadness too; a longing for what might have been, and a fear of what lay ahead. And whilst I missed my father, I really missed the ghost lady, my dearest friend. I had clearly seen her, the last time Dad had abused me, in his bedroom. And then she had vanished, dissolved into the ether, leaving no trace behind. At first, I looked for her everywhere, especially at night. I left the bedroom door open and squinted onto the landing, hoping she might materialise, in her usual spot, with her kind eyes and her layers and layers of fancy skirts.

"Ghost lady," I whispered. "Where are you? Where have you gone?"

I even confided in Tyson, on our walks, thinking perhaps I could conjure her up, by talking about her.

"You'd like her," I told him. "She doesn't talk but she's nice. She's a good listener. Maybe a bit like you, Ty."

I hoped against hope for a glimpse of her, a rustle of her dress, a flash of her smile. But there was nothing. My heart ached to see her again. In many ways, her disappearance hurt me more than the absence of my own father.

14

A Bad Thing

One evening, as I was helping wash the dishes after tea, the phone rang. The way my brother stiffened, as he answered, told me instantly it was Dad on the other end of the line.

"No," he was saying. "Yes. No. Yes."

Then: "She's here, I'll put her on."

He turned to me and said: "Tricia, Dad wants to talk to you. Hurry up, he's not got long."

My tea towel fell to the floor, and I was shocked to hear myself yelling: "No!"

I ran from the kitchen, with my heartbeat thundering loudly in my ears, blocking out all the shouts which followed. The knowledge that my father was on the phone, in the kitchen, was too much for me to cope with. I felt threatened, and scared, as though he could reach down the phone wire and grab me.

Get into my bedroom now!

In my mind, whilst my father had been away, I had sanitised his character into someone who lay on the sofa laughing at Chubby Brown, or occasionally took us swimming or to the zoo or to Blackpool Illuminations. Now he was calling the house, now he was actually, tangibly, on the other end of the phone, his presence reared up against me like a monster. Shaking with terror, I ran into my bedroom and threw myself under the duvet, sobbing.

I could not face him, even on the telephone, and the concern over any punishment for my disobedience was eclipsed by the shock of hearing his voice after so long. All the memories I had fought so hard to bury surged into my mind: the weight of his arm crushing me to the bed, the grotesque, gagging smell of the abuse, his pathetic, self-serving pleas after every abomination:

'It's not my fault, Tricia. Don't tell anyone. You know how scared I am of going to prison.'

In my bunk bed, I lay with my head under the pillow until the noise downstairs had calmed down. I fell asleep and when I woke later, the house was quiet and my father's phone call was thankfully relegated to a long list of domestic problems. Even so, I wondered why he had wanted to talk to me. Perhaps he was coming back home? Maybe the abuse was about to start all over again. Much as I missed him, much as I loved him as a father, I didn't want him living back at home either. My thoughts were mixed-up and muddied and I couldn't make sense of them at all. Just days later, one of my older siblings took me aside and told me Dad had been jailed for four years for the sexual abuse of children.

"You won't see him for a long time," he told me. "He did a bad thing."

It was a matter-of-fact announcement, as was the way in our house with major issues. But again, the words snagged at something in my consciousness, and it was like unpicking a thread, and watching it unravel and unwind. I had a prickly sense that this had happened to me too.

"OK," I replied. "Thanks for telling me."

And that was it. Oddly, my main concern, after hearing about Dad's conviction, was not at all what Dad had done to me; I did not focus on my own trauma. It was rather that Dad, who had always insisted, drummed into me daily, that he was terrified of prison, was now stuck in the very place he dreaded the most.

In my child's mind, this seemed like the most awfully unfortunate coincidence. I wondered if anyone else knew of his prison phobia, or whether Dad would be relying on me to speak out and make his fears known? Day after day, I wrestled with the indecision. I felt I should share what Dad had told me, but had no idea who to confide in, and had no courage to do so. And even if I did, would it make any difference? Who on earth would listen to me? But then, I was scared Dad would be angry with me, for letting him down and allowing him to end up in a prison cell without me even registering so much as a complaint. I worried too, how he was coping, stuck in a place he loathed.

I was eaten up with conflict and contradiction. He was a monster, and yet he was still my dad. Strangely, the two roles were not mutually exclusive, and I didn't like to think of him all afraid and lonely in prison. I remembered his mournful, sunken eyes and thought they would now look sadder still.

As time passed, I began to feel sad and afraid on his behalf, as well as my own. My oversensitivity meant I took on his troubles, or what I imagined were his troubles, in addition to my own.

There was a book in the school library about a burglar, who wore a striped jumper and a mask and eventually landed behind bars for his crimes. I wondered whether Dad had to wear the same uniform, and whether he was locked in a tiny cell, with a concrete floor, and substantial bars at his window too. On the last page of the book, the burglar looked very repentant; I felt a pang at the sight of his sorry face pressed up against the metal bars. I asked myself whether my dad was sorry too. And if he was, could that ever be enough? I was haunted all day and, it seemed, all night.

Most mornings when I woke, I had wet the bed. This was further evidence that my bedwetting was not as a result of seizures, as my father had claimed. I had no idea why I was incontinent at night, but I knew it was linked to the sexual abuse, the misery and the guilt. And wetting the bed, aged 10, just compounded my shame.

Quickly, before anyone else was awake, I stripped the bed, set the washing machine off, and found mismatched clean bedding. I showered obsessively, desperate to get rid of the smell. Bed-wetting was another secret, another burden for me to carry on my young shoulders. And so, even though the abuse and the seizures had stopped, my anxiety festered and bubbled and spread like an eczema through my mind.

A Bad Thing

* * * *

It wasn't long after Dad was jailed when a social worker came to the house, and I was instructed to wash my face, sit on the sofa quietly, and answer her questions. I didn't appreciate the significance of the visit, but I realised it was important. She asked me how I was getting at school and what class I was in. It all seemed quite trivial to me. She didn't ask me about my father, certainly nothing about whether he had sexually abused me too. Baby Expressions was the only one I had ever confided in, and she did not have a voice. My doll could not speak up for me, any more than I could speak up for myself. As a child, the symbolism, and the tragedy of it, was lost on me.

"And do you enjoy school?" asked the social worker. "And what's your favourite subject?"

The questions were innocuous. Even so, thrust into the limelight, I felt a cold sweat trickling down between my shoulder blades and a hot rash itching up my neck and face.

"Well, we'll see you again soon, Patricia," she smiled, as she stood up to leave.

Even before the media picked up news of Dad's conviction, our whole estate seemed to already know his shameful crimes. The outrage locally was quite rightly aggravated because Dad had been a swimming coach, helping out at galas and competitions with many of the kids in the community.

"It's disgusting, that's what it is," snapped one of my neighbours, as I walked Tyson one evening. "Should have thrown away the key."

I nodded, numbly, with my heart racing in panic. As a child, I took her at her word and visualised a prison guard throwing a large, iron key into a bottomless well. This filled me with unease. If they did throw away the key, how would he ever get out? Would he be condemned to prison, the one place which terrified him, for the rest of his life? I remembered Dad using the exact same phrase when condemning child sex offenders himself. Was he willing to accept the same fate he had wished on others?

As I walked to school each morning, I felt a strange cocktail of disgust and sympathy emanating from the mothers on our estate. Some physically shielded their children from me, as though I had the plague, as though my father's disease could somehow be transmitted through me. Others gave me sad smiles and asked how I was, and how my family was coping. But generally that was as far as it went. Some of the parents said to me:

"If you need anything Patricia, you absolutely must let me know."

But I knew, even as a child, they didn't mean it. I was the last person they wanted to hear from. The platitudes were meant to make them feel better, not me. And the children were more direct, more brutal, than their parents.

"Your dad's a nonce, isn't he?" one of my classmates commented. Neither of us knew what the term meant but I realised it was connected with his prison sentence.

"My mum said I've not to play with you," one girl told me, with a glint in her eyes.

I shrugged. This was nothing new.

"But," she added viciously, "I told her I don't come near you anyway because you always have head lice."

My shoulders sagged with resignation as a cackle of amusement vibrated through the group. For me, the head lice presented even more of a problem than my father being a paedophile. It seems absurd now, but as a child, they were my priorities. It was all about surviving, day to day.

At those times, when I felt completely ostracised, Lisa was always there to cheer me up. Though we went to different schools, I saw her most afternoons and every weekend. Her parents treated me no differently after Dad was jailed, except to show me added kindnesses. And even at school, the bullying only went so far. I was labelled as 'one of the Kings' and our family was notorious for causing trouble of one kind or another. The other children were aware of that, so even though I had never been involved in a row in my life, they were careful not to push me too far.

It was one of the few occasions when it served me well to be a member of a big, angry family. My own pressing concerns were the head lice, the grubby uniform, the lack of food in the fridge at home. Those were the worries which kept me awake at night. And it felt somehow fitting that I was plagued with lice infestations, since the schoolyard felt like a jungle sometimes, and I was a small, frightened animal, cowering in the corner, with predators advancing on every side. On sleepless nights, I was tormented by thoughts of my poor rabbits, my hamsters and guinea pigs; cornered, afraid, and alone. Was I, too, destined for a similarly grisly end?

15

Unpaid Debts

One morning, around three months after Dad was jailed, there was a knock at the door. I was just getting my shoes on ready for school, and I opened it hopefully, thinking perhaps it might be a classmate, though not many of the local kids were permitted to knock on our door.

"Yes?" I said, allowing the door to swing wide.

To my alarm, there were two men on the doorstep, neither of whom looked particularly friendly.

"Is your mum in?" one asked.

I shook my head.

"Or what about your dad?"

I shook my head again.

"When are they back? Do you know?"

A third shake of the head. This was a question I'd have liked an answer to myself.

Before they could grill me further, my brother came

hurtling along the hallway behind me and shooed me out of the way.

"Go and brush your teeth or something, you're going to be late," he said.

As I put on my coat and patted Tyson goodbye, ready to leave, I heard arguing and shouting from the doorstep.

"Don't answer the door again," said my brother, as it slammed shut. "Just switch the lights off and stay quiet next time. Those men want money, and they will be back. They will want to come inside, and they'll want to take our stuff. They're not nice men, Tricia. They're bailiffs."

I'd never even heard of a bailiff, it sounded like a type of farmer to me, but I promised my brother I'd follow his instructions. It was only a matter of days before they were back, and this time, I was prepared. I didn't know what they wanted but the knowledge they were not friendly was good enough for me. As the doorbell went, I hurried into the kitchen with Tyson and Bonnie and ushered them under the dining table with me.

"Quiet," I whispered. "The bad men are here."

The house was deathly silent until the letterbox rattled, and a voice shouted: "We know you're in there. Open up!"

The command sent a jolt of alarm right through me. Tyson nuzzled my ear, and I hugged him to me, like a comfort blanket.

"We're OK," I whispered. "Just stay still. No barking."

The bailiffs eventually got fed up and left, and my legs were stiff and sore by the time I crept out from under the table.

"We did it!" I said triumphantly, sneaking a cube of cheese from the fridge for Tyson.

But it was far from over. The debt-collectors kept on coming, every day, banging at the doors and peering in through the windows, until eventually they caught us out as we arrived home from the shops one afternoon.

"Open up!" they demanded, holding out a letter for my older siblings to read.

Within minutes, the men were in the living room, unplugging the telly. My older brothers remonstrated and argued, whilst I stood and stared in open-mouthed astonishment. I had no idea this sort of thing could happen. The following week, the small TV from my parents' bedroom disappeared, so we had no televisions left in the house at all. Another week passed and the cooker went. Then the microwave.

"What next?" I asked. "Will they take my bed? They won't take Tyson and Bonnie will they?"

We became experts at hiding behind furniture with the lights off and the curtains closed, pretending to be out shopping or fast asleep or gone to the moon. Anything to make the wicked bailiffs go away. But it never worked for long.

My older siblings held angry, shouty, phone calls with the companies we owed money to, and I hoped someone might bring the telly back, but they never did. After pay-day, Mum brought bags of food shopping. Now though, of course, we had no method of cooking it. I remember being so pleased with myself for opening a tin of spaghetti hoops with our rusty old tin opener, before realising I had no way of heating them up. One afternoon, I came home from school and my brother said:

"The gas is off. Disconnected."

It didn't register with me at all. I didn't even know what gas was for. But that evening, when I tried to run a bath before bed, my feet plunged into icy-cold water, and I shrieked in protest.

"Boiler's off," my brother explained. "I told you, no gas."

Shivering, I tried to stand in the cold bath long enough to at least have a wash. I was so particular with hygiene, because I was conscious my clothes were grimy and shabby, and I often had head lice. I was still wetting the bed too, and fearful I smelled of urine. I did everything I could to keep myself clean. But with no hot water, it was a struggle. I tried boiling the kettle downstairs and carrying it up, before working out it would take far too long to fill up a bath. I felt sorry for Baby Expressions too; she usually followed me in the bath every evening. I worried about her getting smelly and picking up nits, like me.

"Don't worry," I told her, as I wiped her face with a cold cloth. "I'll find some gas from somewhere. It can't be that difficult."

Living without gas, central heating, hot water, a cooker and a microwave was a major inconvenience for a little girl. But my main gripe was the lack of TV. My favourite cartoon was the 'Ren and Stimpy Show' and it felt like a matter of life and death to miss it. The gas wasn't off for long, and though it was a relief to be able to soak in a hot bath again, I'd much rather have had our telly back.

Lisa's mum was very kind during this time, inviting me for tea and sleepovers, and letting me watch TV programmes with their family. It never ceased to amaze me how Lisa was allowed to casually fling open cupboards and drawers and dig out biscuits or crisps for us both.

"Don't you get into trouble?" I marvelled. "Just helping yourself without even asking permission?"

Even before our most recent crisis, food had always been strictly rationed in our home. I was not usually allowed to even make a slice of toast without getting clearance first from my father. Lisa's house seemed so laid-back and relaxed, to the point where I was unsettled by it. It felt like unbridled decadence to rip open chocolate digestives and polish off half the packet. Mum came home one day with more shopping bags full of food, and, as she was stacking it away in the cupboards, she handed me two tins of beans.

"Here, ask Vi next door if she can heat these up for our dinner," she said.

Vi was our elderly neighbour, living in an old bungalow, a little further up the street. She was a diminutive lady, who always wore a neatly pleated skirt, a soft pastel-coloured cardigan, and had her helmet of bluish hair set weekly in a local salon.

"My mum said can you heat these up please?" I asked sheepishly. "For our dinner."

Vi was a lovely woman but I was so apprehensive, especially when speaking to adults, and each word felt like I was squeezing it through a wringer. By the time I'd finished speaking, my face was covered with a fine film of sweat and my rash was snaking up my neck. To my surprise, Vi looked at the tins with suspicion.

"This is all you're having for your dinner?" she asked. "Have you got someone else heating up the rest of it?"

I shook my head.

"You tell your mother I'm no fool," she said, but she was already hurrying into the kitchen and rustling through the cutlery drawer for a tin-opener.

"Here," she said to me, opening up a biscuit tin. "You help yourself whilst we wait for these beans to boil. You'll need more than beans to make you grow."

One afternoon soon after, Vi stopped me on my way home from school.

"Listen, my love," she said. "I've cooked a big shepherd's pie and an apple crumble, and I need somebody to help me eat them. Will you bring your sisters and brothers round for tea?"

I nodded happily, my mouth watering. Vi and her husband seemed genuinely thrilled to have us as guests, as though we were doing them the favour. They plied us with lemonade and second helpings of pudding, and on our way out, Vi said:

"Same time on Sunday? I'm doing a roast chicken dinner and a rice pudding."

She never once judged us or asked what was going on in our crazy house. Instead, with that old-fashioned sense of community, which is sadly dying, she saw a family in need, and she did something about it herself. Her kindness went far beyond her cooking too. On Saturday afternoons, she'd sometimes spot me hanging around, at a loose end on the street, with Tyson.

"Hey, Patricia!" she called, tapping on her window. "There's a lovely old black and white film about to start. Come on in!"

The films weren't really my sort of thing, there was too much kissing and crying, but any telly was better than none at all. Vi was hard of hearing and she had the TV on full volume. I settled myself on the couch with Baby Expressions at one side, Tyson at the other, and Vi gave me one of her home-made jam tarts.

The film was so loud, the sound bounced from wall to wall and drowned out any conversation between us, which suited me perfectly. I was always worrying people might ask what was going on at home or make a horrible remark about my father. I thought I'd say the wrong thing and land myself in trouble. Vi's television was a sort of safety-net for me; it gave me the perfect escape route from unwanted questions.

"You OK there, my love?" she yelled at the top of her voice, from just three feet away, and I nodded and gave her the thumbs up. I swear I could feel Tyson shaking with a silent mirth next to me.

Vi had a heart of gold, and each time she invited me into her home, I felt as though she had picked me up, out of the sludge of everyday life, and offered me a piggy-back through the worst of it. Those small acts of compassion lifted my spirits, in a way that only small human interactions can. I loved her for it.

Eventually, Mum managed to get hold of a second-hand

cooker. A couple of months later, we got a telly too. Mum was still working long shifts, returning every few days, sometimes just briefly, sometimes staying a little longer. Money was very tight, as always, and our household limped along, like a wounded animal, wondering if this next day might be the last. Again, I thought of my poor pets in the gloomy shed, slaughtered one day at a time. I did not often go to bed hungry, but I existed on snacks, junk food, and assorted tins, going for days without a properly cooked and nutritious meal. There was no time or space for me to feel relief that the sexual abuse from my father was over, because a new trauma had slotted neatly into its place.

I thought back to those mornings when I had crept stealthily past Dad's door, terrified of disturbing him, on my way down to breakfast. On those mornings I had cereal and milk; both at once seemed such a luxury now. On those mornings, my rabbits, hamsters and guinea pigs were waiting, cosy in their cages, for me to feed and cuddle them.

Now the bogeyman was gone. But gone also was the framework of my childhood. I had no food, no routine, no pets. The bodies of my beloved animals lay rotting in an unmarked grave somewhere. As a child, I genuinely could not decide which scenario was worse.

16

Back To School

I was 11 years old by now and preparing to leave primary school. The prospect of the forthcoming summer holidays, packed with new possibilities and fun, should have been a happy one. But I couldn't help fretting about the future, about my new school uniform, my bus pass, my lunch card.

Everything cost money. And we didn't have any. Lisa's mum and Vi were both very kind. But I knew I couldn't possibly ask them to buy me a high school PE kit or a travel pass or a winter coat. I needed school shoes and a bag.

I had learned from my older siblings that I would need a compass, protractor, and scientific calculator. The list seemed endless; insurmountable. I didn't know what I was going to do. I didn't even have a phone number to get hold of my mother, and anyway, I doubted she'd be able to help me.

"Oh Tyson," I groaned, as we walked around the estate.

"How am I supposed to start high school without a uniform? I'll be in trouble on my very first day."

Tyson gave me his customary snuffle and he did his party-piece funny dance, rocking and forth. Somehow, that always made me feel better and I found myself giggling as we walked along. In the last days of my final term at primary school, I won a competition in English, for a story I'd written, and the prize was a trip to a local fast-food restaurant, along with the other winners, to make our own ice-cream sundaes. I couldn't wait. I wasn't used to winning anything or receiving prizes and I was secretly very proud. But as I queued patiently in the restaurant, my teacher said to me:

"I imagine this sort of thing will seem too young and silly for a girl like you, Patricia?"

I hesitated, not really understanding what she was trying to convey. Instead of replying, I bowed my head, relying on my usual tactic of trying to remain invisible.

"I mean, you're not used to decorating ice-creams, you've more important things to worry about," she pressed.

I realised her impression of me was one of a world-weary girl who had already left my childhood far behind, and she was probably quite right. Yet even so, I loved the day out, making sundaes, trying different sweets and sprinkles. It was my only trip out of the entire summer and for a short while, it was a distraction from my worries at home. For a short while, it was my chance to be a child.

The arrival of the warm weather in August helped divert my attention too. Lisa and I played for hours in Bluebell

Woods, picking wildflowers and going through our Spice Girl dance routines in a clearing by the pond.

"I've been practising my cartwheels, like Sporty Spice," I told her, giving a demonstration, a skinny whirl of arms and legs. "Can I do a backflip at the end? Can I? Whilst you're still singing the last verse? Like this?"

We took it all so seriously, as if we were due on stage at Wembley the following night. We rehearsed over and over, until we believed we were faultless. Other days, we played in The Carrs, a huge and picturesque area of parkland in Wilmslow, with the river Bollin running through it. We took our shoes and socks off and paddled in the shallow area, squealing in delight at the ice-cold and hurting our feet on the pebbles. Our favourite part of the river was Red Rock, a sandy section, which had the perfect climbing tree growing out of the side bank.

"Race you up the tree and back," Lisa laughed, and we threw our shoes and socks to the ground and ran, splashing and laughing, to grab the lowest branch.

I was invited to sleep-overs at least once a week, and my older brother never objected. It was probably respite for him, and he at least had one less problem to worry about with me out of the house. And that, sadly, was exactly how I saw myself, and how I had been encouraged to see myself: as a problem.

Sometimes, on the warmer evenings, there was a communal game of rounders, with the local parents digging out their shorts and showing off their pasty legs and rings of middle-aged fat. My father's absence pierced through me like a knife on those nights. Strangely, I remembered only the good things; my father's arms windmilling as he bowled out the opposition's best player, my father laughing with the other dads as they searched for lost tennis balls in the hedges, my father giving me 50p to go to the chip shop with the other kids…

Was he a good man with some bad in him, or a bad man, with some good in him? And what, really, was the difference? Was the bad so very bad that it cancelled out all the good? There was no chart, no calculation to find the correct answer, but even as a little girl, I suspected with a sinking heart that this was the case.

Some crimes were unforgivable. But I clung, regardless, to the blurry and slanted memories of him packing us all in the car and driving to Blackpool or buying me bottles of Fanta in the Spanish hotel. I didn't see the harm in lying to myself, every now and again, to make myself feel better. I just wanted to have a dad.

* * * *

One night, my friends and I got caught in a heavy rain shower, and by the time we got home from the woods, I was soaked through and shivering. Opening the front door, and into the hallway, I was struck immediately by the silence. Usually, Tyson and Bonnie rushed to meet me with excited barks and wagging tails. But the house was empty.

"Where have they gone?" I demanded, calling out. "Where are the dogs?"

There was no reply. I checked each room and searched the garden and then went out into the street, calling their names.

"Tyson, Bonnie!"

But there was no sign of either animal. Even then, in those first few minutes, I had a horrible, defeated, feeling. Tyson was eight years old, and he had never gone missing before. He was a good and loyal dog. And the fact that both dogs had disappeared together made it unlikely there had been an accident with a car or a mishap of some sort. Still in my wet clothes, with my trainers squelching on the flooded pavements, I began knocking on neighbours' doors and checking gardens.

"Sorry, love," Violet said. "I'll keep an eye out, but I haven't seen either of them today."

With a heavy heart, I eventually trudged home, hoping they'd be there to greet me. But the silence was deafening; an assault on my ears, as I stood in the empty hallway.

"Tyson!" I yelled, desperately, forlornly. "Where are you?"

I ripped pages out of an old schoolbook and made flyers and posters. I knew it was pointless, but I also knew I could not sit back and do nothing. Late that night, in between rain showers, I taped my posters to the lampposts and bus stops on the estate.

Lying in bed later, I felt bereft. I listened to the rain slapping against the windows and wondered where Tyson was. I desperately hoped he was warm and dry and safe, but I didn't believe it. I was used to him sneaking in, during the night, and lying on my legs. Or lying, so gently, on my head, if I had a headache. He and I were best pals; he was my friend, my therapist, my confidante.

"Tyson," I sobbed into my pillow.

He was not a particularly big dog but the hole he left in the house was huge. Each room felt so empty and lonely without him. I remembered his silly dance, I pictured him jumping through the window, and my heart broke over and over again. Day after day, I hoped against hope that he and Bonnie might turn up, tails wagging, but they didn't. I never found out where they'd gone, how, or why. All I got in partial and unhelpful explanation was that dogs were expensive, and money was tight. I missed Tyson, especially. He had helped me through such difficult times in my life. And, just as with my rabbits, my guinea pigs and my hamsters, I didn't even get to say goodbye.

My heart ached to see him one last time, to feel his fuzzy nose in my hand, to see his brown eyes widen as I confided my latest problem. Tyson had managed to make me smile on days when I felt all humour had been leached from the world. But without my beloved dog, I feared I'd never laugh again.

* * * *

My angst over my school uniform only got worse as the start date drew nearer. I knew the other kids on the estate already had their school uniforms, their new blazers hanging on the back of bedroom doors, their pristine white shirts and shiny new shoes waiting in their wardrobes. What was I going to do? I felt too ashamed to confide in anyone. Lisa's mum had taken her out shopping and bought everything she needed ready for the transition. She'd also picked out new outfits for her summer holidays, including a pair of trainers which I loved and desperately wanted myself. I felt a tiny stab of jealousy as Lisa paraded her new clothes in her bedroom.

"Yeah, nice," I said glumly, aware I was being ungracious, but feeling too fed up and sorry for myself to paint on a smile.

She had no idea how envious I felt, or I'm sure she'd have gifted me her new clothes, without a second thought. She had such a good heart and I felt bad for feeling so resentful and out of sorts. But my grief over Tyson, added to the worry over my uniform, was dragging me down and I was sick of always being the kid without. A few days before I was due to start at high school, one of my older brothers said to me:

"Come on Tricia, I've got some money for your shoes."

More relieved than excited, I slipped on my jacket and we walked to a shoe-shop on the corner of the high street.

"Choose a pair of shoes and a bag," he said. "Whatever you want. As long as they're not expensive."

He showed me a £20 note in his hand and my heart fluttered a little. Normally, I'd have been over the moon at the prospect of choosing new shoes all by myself, even if they were only school shoes. But somehow, this didn't feel right. I didn't want this level of freedom and choice.

I watched all the parents in the shoe shop, shaking their heads and pursing their lips as their daughters sulkily pointed out patent leather slip-ons with fancy bows. Perversely, that was what I wanted to do. I wanted to choose inappropriate shoes and for somebody to tell me no, for somebody to pick out sensible shoes instead, for somebody to care enough about me starting high school.

"Ok thanks," I said.

My brother went to wait outside the shop whilst I chose a very cheap and conservative pair of shoes and a plain bag, big enough for an A4 folder, just as I'd been told, and generic enough not to stand out and attract any kind of comment. As I queued to pay, I castigated myself furiously at my own lack of reach and ambition. This had been my chance to buy whatever I wanted, and I had spectacularly blown it. Even when choosing shoes, my first priority was to stay under the radar, under the surface, unnoticed. Unloved. I was realising too much freedom could be just as stifling and damaging as none at all.

Back at home, we searched through the wardrobe in my older sister's bedroom before we found her old burgundy school cardigan, a burgundy tie, frayed at the edges, and a grey skirt with a years-old stain on the front. She had no white school shirts in my size so instead, I would have to settle for wearing my brother's old shirts. These buttoned on the opposite side, the wrong side as far as the entire population of the school was concerned, which instantly sent me into a frenzy. I didn't want to be marked out as different in any way. What if the other kids noticed, and they surely would, that I was wearing boys' shirts? I was filled with a liquid dread. My PE kit, again, was faded and worn; cobbled together from hand-me-downs from my older siblings. It had clearly seen better days.

"It'll be fine," Lisa said encouragingly. "Nobody will even notice."

She and I were both moving up to the same high school

and I was looking forward to us being together each day. That first morning, she popped her head round the back door, and shouted:

"Mum said do you want jam on toast? There's plenty."

We both grabbed a slice and set off walking to high school. It was around a half hour walk, and though there was a bus, I didn't have the 50p fare and was too embarrassed to tell Lisa that. Instead, I said:

"Let's walk, it won't take us long, and we've loads of time."

By the time we arrived at school, we were both bubbling over with nervous excitement. It was daunting, walking into the schoolyard, and I pulled my cardigan tightly around me, hoping nobody would notice I was wearing a *boy's* shirt. It felt like an unforgivable faux pas, as far as school etiquette went. I was aware too, of a general smell of mustiness on my clothes; a miasma of stale cigarette smoke and sweat. There was even a lingering scent of dogs, which pulled at my heartstrings.

I edged away from the other kids; in case they picked up on the smell. The last thing I needed was to be singled out and picked on, before my first day had even officially started. But in my anxiety, I began perspiring even more, and the smell got worse. I could feel damp patches forming under my arms and down my back, and my heart sank. My first day was turning into a disaster. Typical. Lisa and I huddled at the edge of a group of girls, and someone piped up:

"Oh, you've got someone else's shirt on! Look at the buttons and the collar! You're wearing a boy's shirt!"

She said it with such incredulity, as though I was wearing a multi-coloured kaftan, as though she simply could not grasp the depths of my stupidity.

How I wished, at that moment, I had a shell to retreat inside, to pull down the blinds, and shut them all out. I felt the rash creeping up around the collar of my boy's shirt and I stared steadfastly at the floor, willing it to open up and swallow me. Then an older boy, a complete stranger, walked past and said:

"Hey, aren't you one of the Kings?"

With my panic intensifying, I nodded, unable to think quickly enough to lie.

"Oh right," he said, smiling. "Well, you need anything, you just shout. Anything at all, you come to me."

My family's reputation for getting into, and winning, fights had, once again, arrived before me, and I had earned a level of immunity by proxy. It seemed foolish me telling people my older siblings didn't ever really notice me and wouldn't have cared much either way if I was teased or picked on at school. But I nodded again and went along with the implicit agreement, and it meant I had no trouble from bullies, or from anyone else. Neither, though, did I have many friends.

Lisa and I were friends of course, and there were a couple of other girls, Penny and Caroline, who seemed to tolerate me for a while, before drifting off to hang around elsewhere. My self-confidence was so low, that after they'd moved on to a new group, I wasn't sure whether they had ever really liked me in the first place. I wasn't sure I really liked me, either. Sometimes, I convinced myself that even my friends only put up with me out of pity, or habit. I found it difficult to find much in common at all with my peer group. At breaktime, the conversation pinballed invariably around such utter trivia, it was almost laughable:

"I've got a gymnastics competition on Sunday, and I'm so nervous."

"Mum says if I get A in my Maths test, she'll buy me those new trainers"

"No way I'm going to ask him out, not with my hair like this. Can anyone lend me any lip gloss?"

I eavesdropped on their conversations with a sort of detached fascination. Their worlds seemed so far away from my own. My particular worries revolved around whether there would be food in the fridge when I got home, or if my uniform would be washed that weekend, or if there'd be screaming rows to keep me awake, as there had the previous night.

One morning, we had no food in at all and I'd gone to school without breakfast. I had no money that day so couldn't buy anything at lunchtime either. And in the middle of an afternoon Geography test, my stomach began rumbling loudly. Everyone else was giggling and looking over their shoulders to try and smoke out the culprit. Terrified of being exposed, I played along, looking over my own shoulder and trying to deflect the sneers elsewhere. It didn't matter so much that I was faint with hunger and dehydration. The main issue was, I just didn't want people to know about it.

I was hiding horrific, mind-blowing, secrets. But as long as nobody found out, I could cope. And so, I felt so much older and wiser than my peers, cowed and bruised by life's hardships, all the last drops of fun and innocence of youth squeezed out of me. It was so hard to fit in. In many ways, I had more in common with my neighbour, little old Vi, than my classmates. And, as a young girl, until he disappeared, I'd had more conversations with Tyson than with anyone else. The realisation brought with it a fresh wave of grief and I bit back my tears as my classmates chatted around me.

My crippling paranoia over head lice grew worse than ever at high school, and I began taking a hairbrush into school each day, hurrying into the girls' toilet block before morning registration, to comb my hair through. Sometimes, I could actually see the lice falling from my hair, onto my shoulders. Watching the miniature specks fall and die was stomach-churning and also rather tragic. Those lice were synonymous with the feelings of misery and shame which dominated my school years. When I had finished picking them out of my hair, I took my cardigan off and shook it hard, unable to suppress a flash of sympathy as they were trampled underfoot on the floor tiles.

"They're only bugs, Trish," I reminded myself. "You can't feel sorry for them."

Even as I walked into class, I was again worrying that my head was itchy, and I had missed one.

"Alright?" Lisa asked with a smile, making space for me next to her on the bench.

I smiled and nodded. Lisa never judged me and never inched away from me, even though she knew all about my scourges of nits. The other kids didn't tease me but neither did they want to be near me. I was an oddity; untouchable both because of my scary siblings and my poor personal hygiene.

* * * *

As the first term of high school came to an end, the weather turned bitterly cold. The wind, as I walked to school each day, seemed to whip right through my school cardigan. One morning, as I stood in the school yard, with my teeth chattering and my fingers white with cold, my head of year called me indoors.

"Here, Patricia," he said, handing me a black coat. "This looks about your size and it will keep you warm. Might not be the latest style, but it's better than nothing."

I was so surprised by his compassion; it took me a few moments to find my voice and thank him. And when I did, the words caught in my throat, and I was mortified to feel a stray tear rolling down my cheek.

"You're a good girl, Patricia," he said with a smile. "Keep going, just as you are. You're doing well at high school."

My form teacher was always kind to me too. I was glad of it, but I also wondered how, and what, she knew about my problems. Was I in some way marked out, invisibly, as a child with trauma? Was it the head lice, the shabby uniform, the blank expression? Did she know about my father being in jail? The thoughts, flitting around my head like trapped wasps, filled me with absolute dismay and humiliation. Had she spotted me as a child in need, or had I been brought to her attention by someone else, and who was that? I would never know the truth and in any case, I was classified as being different, peculiar, and vulnerable, which was precisely what I didn't want. More than anything, I wanted to fit in. But it seemed the harder I tried, the more I stood out.

In year seven, we had weekly Food Tech lessons, which necessitated us bringing ingredients in from home. Of course I never had them ready. Occasionally, the cookery teacher had spare ingredients, but again, I hated being singled out in class, all the focus on me, like a charity case, as she palmed me off with someone else's extra flour and a borrowed egg. I felt like the *Little Match Girl* from the fairy tale; poor and helpless – and, worst of all, pitied.

"Here," she said, handing me a donated cooking apple, to make apple pie. "I'm sure I can pinch some pastry mix from somewhere too."

She was trying to help but I found it demeaning and degrading. I just wanted to be allowed to crawl under the table, as I had as a small child, and wait until it was all over. One week, we were given the ingredients list for a fruit cocktail, and this time, I was really keen to take part and be the same as everyone else. It sounded fun to make, but more than that, I just wanted to be one of the crowd. I bounded in through the front door, and luckily cobbled together some loose change to go to the greengrocers nearby. I realised I'd forgotten my cookery list when I arrived at the shop and so picked up the cheapest fruit – a box of hard, unripe plums – and skipped home. I couldn't wait for Food Tech the following day.

"Got my stuff," I told the teacher with a smile.

When the teacher saw the plums, she frowned a little but said, with a false brightness: "Well, you could give them a go, I suppose. Pop them in the mixer when you've washed them."

As I threw them into the blender, I thought again of my teacher's frown, and I had a crisis of confidence. Moments later, I realised it was well-founded. As I poured the mixture out of the blender, it slopped into a glass; a viscous pile of dark purple sludge. The unripe plum skins had not blended well at all and looked like lumps of mud in the mix. There were a few giggles, a few snorts of disgust. We were all supposed to take a straw and drink our cocktails there and then, but my mix was so gloopy, I couldn't even suck it up the straw.

"Oh, Patricia," said my teacher sadly, as though this was all she could ever expect of me, as though this absolutely summed up my cookery career so far.

When it was time to clear away, I chucked the lot into the bin. That was the first and last time I had my own ingredients and it had gone so terribly wrong. Perhaps, as my dad had always said, it was my fault; it was always my fault. I didn't seem to be able to get anything right.

17

A New Look

In my first year at high school, I had a routine hospital check-up.

"No fits?" asked the doctor, scanning my notes with a smile. "Looks like you're doing really well, Patricia. The improvement is remarkable."

In truth I hadn't had a single seizure since Dad left. This could have been because the sexual abuse had stopped, and it could have been because Dad had been fabricating most of the seizures. It was most likely a combination of the two, but I knew better than to tell the doctor any of that.

"I feel much better," I managed to say, before blushing crimson.

I had hoped he might cancel all of my medication completely, as I'd requested in my letter, but he explained it was better to reduce it gradually, and he agreed he'd recommend a lower dosage, to see how I got on. It was a move in the right direction, and I was pleased, though I couldn't wait to get rid of the dragging, fuggy feeling that seemed to press me down, like a heavy rain cloud, each day. I blamed the medication for that.

"Whatever you're doing, keep it up," said the doctor, at the end of the appointment. "You look really well."

At school, too, I was making steady progress. My attendance was good, because my health was better, and because my father wasn't around to insist I pulled regular sickies. Paradoxically, my school attendance had improved with no adult influence. I still didn't enjoy my lessons, I felt absolutely out of my depth, and I wasn't ever fully comfortable with children my age. I had a lot of grown-up worries, which they just couldn't have understood. But at least I was in school, every day, and I was doing my best.

Towards the end of year 7, like many of the kids of my age, and of my generation, I got hooked on MSN messenger. At school, we were all obsessed and it was all we ever talked about. Penny, one of the girls I was quite friendly with, had a computer in her bedroom, and to my surprise – and delight – she invited me round one evening.

"Fancy chatting to some boys later?" she asked. "I've told my mum we've got a school project and we're working together."

I was thrilled to be chosen. I told myself it was because she really liked me. Looking back, I suspect she realised I was desperate to fit in, and she also knew I had no framework of rules or discipline at home. It didn't matter if I stayed out late, chatting to strangers in strange houses. Nobody would notice.

"Yeah," I beamed. "I'd love to."

"See you at about 7pm," Penny said.

I arrived at her house in Handforth, a 40 minute walk away, carrying my school books, as a cover for our story about the project.

"I see you're well prepared," her mum smiled. "Penny's upstairs, waiting for you, love."

"Thanks," I replied. "I can't wait to get started on this geography project."

I felt a brief pang of shame at the lie tripping so easily from my lips but forgot all about it when Penny logged in and the screen lit up. MSN was thrilling because it was new, it was grown-up, and it was illicit. I was not normally a rule-breaker, but this felt anonymous and risk-free; they were just faceless entities on the other side of a chat stream. It was a way of keeping out of the spotlight, yet being amongst all the excitement too, so it was perfect for me.

That night, a Friday, we got chatting to two boys from Stoke-on-Trent. They told us they were 17 years old. Penny and I raised silent eyebrows at each other; we were both still just 12. To us, they were men; a different species entirely.

'Can we meet you tomorrow?' they asked.

My automatic reply was absolutely not.

"Can't," I replied. "Busy."

"Go on," they wheedled. "Be fun. Just for a laugh. We won't do anything. Promise."

The persuasion went on and on and eventually, I felt myself being worn down, my insistence softening and eroding like sand in the rain.

"What do you think?" Penny asked. "Might be fun, Trish. What harm can it be?"

We already knew her mum would be out for most of the following day; she worked Saturdays in a local cake shop. Penny's older brother had left home, and her dad wasn't about. And so, Penny had the house all to herself.

"Nobody would ever know," she added.

I could feel myself swaying further. Like most 12 year olds, we were easily led and easily influenced, and me more than most. By the end of the evening, we had caved in.

"See you tomorrow," said the boys. "Can't wait."

Saturday morning came, and I was a whirl of excitement and misgivings. I set off to Penny's after breakfast; I had no bus fare and so again made the 40-minute walk, as quickly as I could. But I kept changing my mind all the way there; each crisis of confidence colliding with the next.

"Penny, I'm not sure about this," I announced, rapping on her door. "Should we still go? What do you think? Should we wear make-up? Can you lend me a top?"

"Yeah, we've said we'll do it, we can't back out now," Penny said, chewing her lip. "But I know what you mean, I feel a bit funny about it as well."

We had lip gloss and perfume, and Penny found some mascara in the bathroom. We did each other's hair and make-up, got dressed into crop tops and leggings, and set out to the train station to meet the boys. We waited on a bench on the platform at Handforth station in a giggling heap.

"What if they're really awful?" Penny whispered. "Should we just make a run for it? Or pretend we haven't seen them?"

My stomach was somersaulting. I couldn't wait to see them, yet I was nervy too. The train pulled in and two young men stepped off.

"Wow, they are so much older than I thought," I exclaimed. "They're real…men! They're…men, Penny!"

The observation just made us giggle even more. We took the boys back to Penny's road, crouching low behind walls and hedges before making a dash for it into her house when the coast was clear.

"In, in," she said, herding them along, before a neighbour spotted us.

The atmosphere, once inside, was awkward. It was one thing chatting on MSN but face to face we found we had little to say to each other, and Penny and I were both paralysed by attacks of giggles, which kept on coming in waves. The boys were completely straight-faced, which just made us laugh all the more. Eventually, we pulled ourselves together and Penny flicked the TV on and handed round some crisps. We sat, stiffly and politely, like four china figurines on the sofa.

"I really like you," one of the boys murmured, and I felt my heart race as I gave what I hoped was my most alluring smile.

Slowly, I felt a hand inching across my back and down, conscious the same was happening to Penny at the other end of the couch. The kiss, when it came, was mind-blowing. I had never kissed a boy before, not properly, and it was both disgusting and sensational. It lasted so long that afterwards my lips felt slightly numb and rubbery, and I had another fit of the giggles just thinking about it.

After the kissing, things just got more awkward. Penny was on tenterhooks in case her mum finished work early and turned up. She paced to and from the window like a caged animal, straightening cushions and brushing the crisp crumbs into the bin. I, on the other hand, was very keen to clean my teeth.

"You'd better go," we said to the boys eventually. "You'll miss your train. You don't want to be stuck here."

We smuggled them out of the house like fugitives, with hasty directions back to the station, before going back inside and resuming our helpless giggling on the sofa.

"I can't feel my lips," Penny laughed.

"Me neither," I chuckled.

It was our first real experience of boys, and, despite the age gap, it should have been nothing more than innocent fun. It hadn't gone beyond a snog on the sofa, after all. Penny handed me a glass of cordial, to try to get some sensation back into our lips, and said:

"That was my first kiss ever. Was it yours?"

I nodded shyly.

"Maybe it gets better the more you do it," she reasoned. "Next time won't be so bad."

On my way home, bursting to share my news, I did a detour and knocked at Lisa's house.

"I kissed him!" I announced when she opened the door. "I met a boy off MSN, and I kissed him! Like, a proper kiss!"

Giggling, I gave her a blow-by-blow account of the incident, including the rubbery lips, which I was beginning to fear might be permanent.

"Imagine having a real boyfriend," Lisa said dreamily. "Imagine – uugh – having to go all the way, you know? I don't fancy it."

She made a jokey gagging noise, and I suddenly felt my good mood slosh right out of me. I felt horribly cold and sick and distant.

'Don't tell anyone, Tricia, it's not my fault.'

'Take your pyjamas off and do as you're told.'

'Bend over, as far as you can.'

I ran my hands down my face, to try and close off the memories. I couldn't let them out, not now. It just wasn't safe. I thought of my friend, the ghost lady, and wished she could be with me. She was the only witness to my suffering. The only one who knew, the only one who understood. How could I ever begin to share any of that with Lisa, or anyone else?

"No," I croaked eventually. "You're right. It all sounds so gross. I don't fancy it either."

* * * *

By the time I reached the end of year eight, in July 2001, Mum was working slightly more sociable hours and we were settling back into some sort of routine. We had a cranky old cooker and one replacement television, and we were no longer being harassed by bailiffs and debt-collectors. But despite her being around a little more, she was still working long hours at two jobs, money was tight as always, and the house limped along amidst the usual chaos and disarray. There were arguments over the breakfast table, scuffles over missing money or loud music or because someone had used the last of the loo roll. It was exactly as it had been before. But at the same time, it was completely different.

There was no word from Dad, no letters or calls. I'd no idea if he was still in prison or not. I tried not to think of him because it triggered so much conflict and turmoil in my 13-year-old mind. Still, irrationally, I felt a duty to try to get him out of prison, because he had specifically confided in me how frightened he was of being behind bars.

I felt as though he had given me one task, to make sure he stayed out of jail, and I had failed him. I believed the responsibility, like the blame, was on me, and not on him. I presumed, too, he wouldn't be in prison forever and was worried how angry he might be when he was finally released. Would he come and find me? Would the abuse start again, as if nothing had changed? Again, I was torn; I wanted to see him; he was my father. Yet simultaneously, I never wanted to see him again.

At 13, I didn't understand that a four-year prison sentence did not mean four years in prison, and by then, my father was already out, a free man, and living a whole new life. The irony of him celebrating his freedom, whilst I fretted about him stuck in a cell, appals me now.

Dad moved on, and left his family, and the efficient destruction of it, behind him. With his trademark arrogance, he just walked away from the car-crash reality he had created for me. But even if I had known all of that, I think I would still have missed him, a little. It was not a black and white situation, and I could not help my feelings. At 13, I was a child, and I needed my parents.

My father was a bad man. But he had taught me to swim and he had taken me on my one and only holiday to Spain. I remembered him buying me the big bag of Maltesers at the airport and I softened towards him. In the same thought, I reminded myself I was no longer being abused, no longer being groomed or bullied or exploited. In my heart, I was glad he was gone. Yet I felt such guilt for admitting it. This yo-yo worrying was typical of me, I knew that. Typical of me to be scared of water. Typical of me to be frightened by the bugs in the swimming pool. Typical of me to want my father in jail. Typical of me to want him freed.

'Tricia, nobody likes a whiner. Stop making a fool of yourself…'

Following the end of year eight, the summer holidays arrived, and as usual, I spent most days playing out with the other kids on the estate. Inevitably, we spent less time practising dance routines and picking flowers in the woods and more time trying on make-up and clothes. It was just wonderful not to be in school, and to see those weeks of school-free bliss, stretching out, to the horizon and beyond.

Those six weeks felt deliciously endless. At home too, my life improved dramatically, when one of my brothers started dating a local hairdresser called Claire. She was the most glamourous woman I had ever met; her make-up and hair were always perfect, and she had beautifully manicured nails. She wore lots of rings and big, hooped earrings and when she walked past, I caught a waft of an impossibly sophisticated perfume. I was mesmerised, every time she came round to the house. Better still, instead of shooing me away as most of my brothers' girlfriends did, or staring right through me like I wasn't there, she was really friendly and chatty.

My hyper-sensitivity picked up only positive signals from her every time she spoke to me. It was hard for me to believe, but I actually thought she might genuinely like me. Automatically, she called me Trish, like my friends, and not Tricia, as my family did. I told myself it was a secret sign; a code between us, that she was on my side.

"How are you enjoying the holidays?" she asked me, with a sparkling smile. "Have you got lots of plans?"

"Not really," I told her. "I love being off school but there's not much to do around here. I just hang around with my pals."

A few days later, Claire said to me: "Listen, Trish, would you like to come into the salon one day?" she asked. "My treat."

My eyes widened in astonishment. I'd never been to a hairdresser in my entire life. Every time I saw one of my classmates coming into school with a fancy new haircut, I felt a twinge of envy. I always wished, just once, that could be me. My own fair hair had always been long and stringy; dulled through a lack of care and countless nit infestations. More often than not, I scraped it back into a ponytail and prayed no nits would crawl out onto my neck whilst I was sitting in class. That was my personal definition of a good hair day. It was a low-bar, and I was aware of that.

"Yes please!" I beamed. "I'd love to."

Later that week, I found myself outside the salon where Claire worked. I had been so looking forward to the appointment, but as I pushed open the door, and was engulfed by a cloud of expensive and luxurious scents, my confidence suddenly evaporated. It looked, and smelled, so swanky and professional. I didn't belong here. What was I thinking of? With my head down, I shuffled towards the counter, hoping there had been some terrible mistake and Claire would simply turn me around and send me home. Instead, she beckoned me over to an empty chair, and said:

"I've got some great ideas for your hair! Are you happy for me to take charge? Spring a nice surprise on you? What do you think, Trish?"

I nodded, numbly, still overawed.

"You're going to look fabulous, I promise," she replied. "You have such a pretty face, Trish. And gorgeous big eyes! You just need the hair to go with it."

My mouth gaped. I couldn't believe she was speaking to me. Nobody had ever told me I was pretty before. Certainly not gorgeous. Transfixed, I waited, like a little Eliza Doolittle, as my hair was highlighted, washed, trimmed and blow dried. Claire massaged various oils and serums into my scalp, humming and chatting as she went along. After plugging in the hairdryer, for the final stages, she spun my chair away from the mirrors so I couldn't see the transformation.

"We'll do a big reveal at the end," she announced.

When the moment came, I could hardly contain myself. Claire swung me back, in front of the mirror, and I was dumbfounded. The girl who was gawping back at me looked nothing at all like me. My hair was shaped into a cute bob, curled out at the bottom, with striking blonde highlights.

"Well?" she asked, but my wide smile said it all.

"Oh, I love it!" I gasped. "Thank you! I love it!"

I bounced out of the salon, with my hair swinging, and a soaring sense of confidence and happiness. I felt certain, as I walked down the street, that every passer-by, every driver stuck in traffic, would be equally as impressed as I was with my new look.

For 13 years, I'd been hiding myself away, with my head down, battling to stay under wraps. But now, like a butterfly, leaving a chrysalis behind, this was my moment. I was ready to fly.

* * * *

"Wow, Trish!" shrieked Lisa, running up my street to meet me. "I've been sitting in the square, looking out for you coming home. You look amazing. Beautiful! So different! You look – Wow!"

Normally a direct compliment, even from Lisa, would leave me crumbling, collapsing, sinking into my collar. But this time, I accepted it with a smile.

"I like it," I told her happily. "You're right, I am different. Inside, as well as out. I can't explain it. I don't feel like myself at all."

And at home, I was half-surprised, as I opened my front door, when my brother smiled and said: "Hello, you look nice."

"I didn't think you would recognise me," I replied. "I can't get over how strange I feel. I even smell different."

And it was true, the scent of the salon and all the fancy products on my hair was sophisticated and feminine. That evening, Lisa knocked on my door, out of puff, lugging a bulging binbag behind her.

"My mum sent these clothes for you," she announced. "I've carried them all the way. I've outgrown them, and you're smaller than me. If you don't want them, chuck them away, no problem."

I dived into the binbag excitedly, holding up shiny tops, colourful leggings, black jeans, a denim jacket, an almost new pair of trainers, and a beautiful bracelet. Lisa was a good few inches taller than I was, and a little heavier too. But I knew she and her mum had donated far more than a few cast-offs. This was their characteristically generous way of making sure I had the outfits to match the hair.

"Thanks, Lisa," I smiled. "I'll wear them all. They're fabulous."

That night, I lay with my head rigidly still on the pillow, afraid of kinking my hair or losing the wonderful, bouncy shape. The next morning, I was up early. I felt an infectious energy, courtesy of my new bouncy style, and I wanted to pack as much as I could into my day. It was both disconcerting and amazing, getting dressed into someone else's clothes, and brushing someone else's hair. I felt removed from my old self in a way I couldn't explain, but which I really rather liked. I caught sight of myself in the bathroom mirror and the shock rippled through me all over again.

"I can't believe it's you," I told myself, flicking my hair as I pursed my lips in the mirror.

And the metamorphosis went far deeper than the superficial changes in my hair and wardrobe. The transfiguration gave me an edge and a self-assurance, which was at once unsettling and thrilling. Old Tricia had gone for good, and I knew I wouldn't miss her one bit. Sadly, I didn't think anyone else would either.

18

Playing Truant

Idly daydreaming in class, I twirled my lovely highlighted blonde hair around my fingers and wished I was elsewhere. Anywhere but school. I hated algebra; I couldn't work it out and, for the first time in my life, I questioned why I should have to.

Just a few days into year nine, I felt the early stirs of teenage rebellion. Throughout my first two years at high school, I had strived to remain inconspicuous and invisible, always determined not to encourage any kind of fuss. I did my work, and my homework, and my grades were bordering on acceptable.

Because of all the time off I'd had during primary school, I would always be a little way behind with my learning and my work was on the poor side of average. It was never enough to set me apart in class, but it was enough to hold me back from doing well, which was exactly what I wanted. But if ever my grades dipped further, and I failed an assignment, I was filled with guilt and remorse, as though my poor result was all my own fault.

I was miserable with the knowledge that I was a burden in the class; an inconvenience and a problem my teachers could well do without. And yet, I never spoke of it. In fact, I hardly ever spoke at school. I followed the rules, I stared at my shoes, and hoped that would be enough. Yet, as I sat in algebra that day, and the teacher's voice droned on in the background, I felt a mild irritation. Those first seeds of dissent were sown, right there. I was kicking back for the first time ever. At break time, I found Penny by the cloakrooms, and complained:

"I'm so sick of school. I didn't understand a word in maths. I'm behind already and we've only been back a few days. No way I'm sitting in class every day till half-term. I'm just not doing it. I don't even learn anything."

She looked at me in surprise. This wasn't like me at all.

"What have you got in mind?" she asked.

The idea of playing truant had never even occurred to me before; it wasn't something the old Tricia would ever have considered. But she was gone, and, as it turned out, the Trish with the new hairdo and the new clothes did quite fancy a bit of truancy and shopping.

"Yes!" I exclaimed. "Shopping sounds fun! Let's do it. Tomorrow. Let's skip school. We could go into town, try on some clothes, get a burger. Anything's got to be better than doing more algebra."

Penny stared at me and laughed.

"Are you kidding?" she asked. "What's brought this on? Aren't you bothered about getting into trouble?"

"Nah," I said firmly, flicking my new hair. "Let's do it."

So the following morning, instead of walking to school, Penny and I met on the main road and caught the bus to Stockport town centre. I had £3.50 to last the day, so I spent 50p on the bus, leaving me with enough to buy some food and my fare home. As we took our seats on the top deck, I felt a rush of nervous butterflies. Was it obvious? Did the bus driver know we were skipping school? Did he even care?

I wrapped my coat around me and pulled the sleeves over my hands to hide my school uniform. I was glad now of the coat my teacher had given me, far too big, and easily hiding my clothes underneath it. The old Tricia would have been crippled with guilt, remembering the teacher's kindness, and knowing how disappointed he'd be to see me here, on the top deck, going the opposite direction to school. But the new Trish batted that thought away.

"Everyone skips school," I told myself. "I just need to make sure we don't get into trouble."

A prickle of hyper-vigilance ran through my veins as I examined all the faces on the bus, wondering which one was most likely to confront us and ask us why we weren't at school. I worried we might bump into someone we knew, or someone who knew our teachers. I convinced myself I was no longer bothered about doing the wrong thing, but still, I didn't want to get caught.

"It's fine," I said to Penny eventually, after scanning each passenger. "Nobody's even noticed us. Nobody's bothered."

We arrived at Stockport precinct and for the first hour we walked aimlessly up and down the same row of shops, pausing every few minutes and checking our reflections in shop windows, to apply and reapply our fruity lip gloss. During alternate applications of lip gloss, we topped up on our favourite 'So?' body spray. That morning alone, I probably went through a full tube of lip gloss and a can of body spray. Neither of us had any idea why we were going through such a stringent beauty routine; there was nobody else around except us. It was just what 13-year-old girls did.

At lunchtime, we bought a 99p burger each, with a drink. That, too, was nerve-racking, I worried the assistant might challenge us and ask us why we weren't in school. What if she spotted our school badge, on the jumper, and called school? What if she was married to one of our teachers? My mind was running away with increasingly ridiculous possibilities. As it was, she didn't even make eye contact, never mind conversation. Again, we were safe. This was all so much easier than I'd expected. It was a depressing lesson I was learning over and over in life; people didn't care as much as I might have thought. We found a sunny spot on the benches and Penny leaned back, closed her eyes, and said, through a mouthful of burger:

"Aw, Trish, this is the life."

At that moment, I spotted a group of teenage boys walking towards us. They were in school uniform, clearly playing truant, just like us.

"Penny!" I spluttered. "Look!"

As she sat up straight, I fumbled my pungent-smelling body spray and lip-gloss out of my bag and we both ran through an accelerated version of our beauty regime. By the time the boys arrived, we had choked back the rest of our burgers and we smelled sensational. There was room for us all on the benches if we squeezed up tight and it was such fun, chatting and flirting in the sunshine, pursing our lips and thanking our lucky stars for fruity lip gloss.

The afternoon flew by, much faster than it ever did in school, and it was soon time to get our bus home, to keep up the pretence to our families that we'd been in class all day.

"See you again?" the boys asked.

"Yeah sure," I grinned. "Same time next week?"

It had all been so laughably simple and straightforward. The following week, we met with the boys, and it was the beginning of a new routine. We started taking one day a week off school, to walk around the precinct and lavish ourselves with lip gloss and body spray.

We were careful not to miss too many lessons, so as not to arouse suspicion, and the plan went like clockwork. We seemed to get away with it very easily. Sometimes, on our weekly jaunts, we bought a burger, other times we indulged in a Greggs sausage roll. We loved meeting up with different groups of boys.

From afar, my alter-ego watched myself chatting and laughing, flicking my hair back and smiling with my shiny lips. It was like looking at a complete stranger. I couldn't fathom where all my confidence and nerve had come from. We'd read the story of Samson in Religious Education lessons, and like him, I was drawing my strength and character from my hair. It was as though my new hairstyle had brought with it a whole new personality; it was all part of the package.

"Hey, thank you," I heard myself giggling, as one of the boys paid me a compliment. "You're not so bad yourself."

I had spent my entire childhood with my head in the sand, hiding away from the light like a nocturnal animal. Now, it was time to take some chances and climb out, above the surface. It was time to have some fun.

* * * *

Penny and I were happily reapplying our lip gloss one afternoon, staring in a shop window, when we noticed two police officers walking straight towards us.

"Oh no," I breathed. "What do we do?"

Time seemed to stand still as the officers, one male, one female, got nearer. And nearer. Though my mind was in overdrive, churning out different options, I couldn't think of a single way to avoid them.

"Maybe they're not coming for us," Penny whispered. "Maybe they'll just walk straight past."

But I just knew they were. I didn't need hyper-senses to know we had been well and truly spotted.

"Hello," said the female officer, sounding friendly enough. "Can I ask why you're not both in school?"

"Had a hospital appointment, my friend came with me, we're going back to school now," I heard myself babbling. "In fact, we're on our way to the bus stop. Look, we're in uniform. We're definitely going."

The officer smiled and took out her notebook.

"Names and addresses please," she said.

"Patricia King," I replied.

Penny's voice wobbled as she gave her name and address.

"You girls get straight back to school now please," said the officer. "I presume this is your bus stop, just along the street?"

We nodded and, as the officers watched, we walked to the stop, giggling nervously.

"Oh, that was close," I stuttered. "God, imagine if they tell school. What will we do?"

"Imagine if they tell my mum!" Penny groaned.

On the bus home, we were both quiet and crestfallen, shaken up by our first brush with the law. But over the next few days, my mood slowly turned full circle. We had been stopped by the police, and we had gotten away with it! We had sweet-talked them, and they had fallen for it! There were no repercussions at all. I felt brighter, bolder, more confident, than ever before.

We continued our routine of missing one, maybe two days a week and began meeting up with a group of boys at an arcade in Parrswood, Manchester. They had more money than us, enough for a steady supply of burgers, chips, drinks and bags of sweets. We hung around the shops, played on slot machines and trailed up and down the same rain-splattered, grey streets. It was repetitive and mundane and the weather was often chilly. But it was so much better than going to school. One afternoon, preoccupied with our beauty routines, we spotted a police officer crossing over the road, heading right for us.

"Oh no," Penny muttered.

"Leave it to me," I said, under my breath.

"Why aren't you girls in school?" he asked.

"Afternoon off," I explained. "It's exam week, you see. We get time off as a reward."

I pulled my coat around me to hide the school badge on my jumper. The last thing I needed was him calling school to check. He looked at me sceptically.

"Names please," he said.

"Leanne Turner and Sarah Daly," I replied, without missing a beat.

I rattled off a false address too, giving Penny's on the same fictitious street as mine. I felt her bristling with indignation, next to me.

"Where did that come from?" she gasped, as we walked away. "You lied, you actually lied, to a police officer, Trish! What the hell has happened to you?"

I grinned and flicked my hair.

"I have no idea," I said proudly.

And that was the truth. I had spent so many years in complete and reverent obedience. Now, I was so keen to make up for lost time, I was going overboard. I felt like a runaway train; I couldn't stop myself, but then, neither did I want to.

"Loosen up Penny," I grinned, as I reapplied my lip gloss. "We won't get caught. Trust me."

We were always careful not to miss school two days in a row, so as not to alert our teachers. My form teacher called home, occasionally, to report my absences, but often the line was disconnected, because nobody had paid the bill. And if they did get through, whoever answered was never particularly interested in me missing a day or two from school.

I think in the end the teachers gave up and wrote me off

as being: "One of the King family," as if my abject failure was just what they had expected all along. Well, I thought wretchedly, I'd give them the satisfaction of being right. One morning, I was about to take my epilepsy medication, after breakfast, and I felt a sudden jab of resentment.

"No!" I said firmly, out loud.

In triumph, I shoved the blister pack back into the box.

"I'm not taking them," I muttered. "Ever again."

The only question was why I hadn't thought of this sooner. I had stopped following the rules. I had stopped being the old Tricia. Now it was time to stop taking my pills too. I remembered the doctors said it was safer to reduce the dosage gradually. But I wasn't bothered. With a grim satisfaction, I replaced the packet back on the shelf with the others piles of medication. Tegretol and Carbamazepine, alongside my inhalers and indigestion remedies, seemed to stare back at me accusingly.

"Don't care," I mumbled. "I'm done with tablets."

The days turned into weeks, and I never wavered. I didn't take a single pill. I half expected some sort of major medical fall-out from my recklessness. Perhaps I'd have an almighty seizure which would land me in hospital. Maybe I'd suffer severe withdrawal symptoms. But there was nothing.

More time passed, and I thought that surely someone in my family would notice I wasn't taking my medication. But sadly, probably predictably, nobody did. I was almost hopeful I might be confronted by a pile of unused Tegretol boxes, as I came in from school one afternoon, and a concerned family member demanding an explanation. But nobody commented. Nobody seemed to care. In a funny way, it was a disappointment to get away with it so easily.

Again, as with the truancy, I was learning that people really didn't care about me as much as I might have hoped. As the last traces of the drugs left my system, I was, at least, looking forward to some respite from the horrible side-effects. But though the drowsiness and fuzziness lifted a little, the feelings of apathy and a general heaviness still remained. I was no longer nauseous and sickly, but I had a knot of anxiety in my stomach which felt worse even than before. It seemed my medication was not entirely to blame for my dark moods and again, my mind wandered back to my father; the bogeyman whose legacy was to leave a lasting curse on my life.

I had not seen him or heard from him now for nearly five years. Sometimes, I struggled to remember quite how he looked, the exact tone of his voice, the way he held himself when he was walking. Yet in my dreams, those memories came to me, as sharp and painful as shards of broken glass. In nightmares, I visualised perfectly the sunken eyes, the heavy arm, the wide neck. I remembered the stifling, smothering terror, the stench of the abuse. I would never escape that. Never.

One morning, fuddled with kaleidoscope flashbacks from my dreams, I stumbled downstairs, into the kitchen, and looked at the pile of unused epilepsy medication on the shelf. Suddenly, I heard a clear, authoritative voice in my head. It was neither Tricia, nor Trish, yet it was unmistakably my own.

"You could swallow all of this at once," said the voice. "Take the packets, find a quiet spot by the railway line, and take the lot. It could all be over for you. That simple."

19

Pushed to the Edge

Our homework, for English one weekend, was to write an essay, and inwardly, I groaned at the prospect. I hated writing, I hated English, I hated school.

"You have three choices of title," said our supply teacher, as she handed out the sheets. "I'd like you to consider structure and organisation. Write a plan. I want you to use lots of imagery and adjectives. If possible, I'd like you to rely on a real event, something which happened to you. Make it personal."

I stared at the options.

'My Life Story.'

'The Holiday.'

'The Visitor.'

I had no interest whatsoever in writing about any of these.

My intention was to dash off half a page of work with the minimum of effort.

"What essay are you going to choose?" Lisa asked, as we walked home.

"Dunno," I shrugged.

"You could do a holiday, you know, the time you went to Spain with your dad?" she suggested. "I think I'll write about my holidays."

It was pitiful that the only holiday I'd had was nearly six years ago. And I suspected again, as I had then, that the trip to Spain was more of a bribe than a treat. That night, everyone was out, and I had the house to myself. I felt listless and unsettled, walking from room to room. Mention of the holiday had brought back a barrage of unwanted memories of my father. I couldn't bear to look at the armchair in the living room. Nor could I bring myself to look outside at the shed, where my precious pets had lived – and died.

With my head pounding, I went upstairs to lie on my bed. My thoughts drifted towards Tyson, and the way he would always intuit when I was sad or in pain. I remembered how, when I had a headache, he used to lie next to me, his head gently resting on mine, as if he could osmotically draw out my pain.

"Miss you so much, Ty," I mumbled.

My sadness gave way to anger. I wanted Tyson back. I wanted my childhood back. I wanted something to change. I sat up and grabbed my English book and a pen from my bag.

'This is my life story,' I wrote. 'I've never dared share

this before. Never said it out loud, nor wrote it down. I'm trembling as I write each word…'

I hadn't intended at all to write about the abuse. It wasn't even uppermost in my mind. Yet after thinking about Tyson, and the Spanish holiday, I found I was crackling with hurt and resentment. Like a river, bursting its banks, I flooded each page with my pain and anguish.

Once I started, I couldn't stop. I couldn't redivert the flow. I wrote a first-person account of the barbaric deaths of my rabbits, my hamsters, my guinea pigs and their cute little babies. I wrote about Dad's bedroom and the horrors inside it. I recounted too, the hellish details of what took place in the living room, behind the stained-glass door. I remembered how the ghost lady, Baby Expressions and Tyson were my only support.

'I don't know how I have survived this,' I wrote. 'I have been pushed right to the edge.'

On Monday morning, with a strange sense of calm and acceptance, I handed my essay in. Deep down, I knew I'd have to expect a reaction. I was poking at a sleeping giant. I didn't know what I was hoping for. Perhaps I just wanted something, anything, to happen. I had lit the fuse and now, all that remained was for me to sit and wait for the explosion. The supply teacher gathered all the papers and glanced at my first paragraph but gave nothing away in her facial response.

"You will receive these back at the end of the week," she said. "Anyone not achieving a pass will be required to repeat the essay."

Repeating the assignment was the least of my problems. I

barely slept that week. I half-expected the police might come to the house to question me. I wondered whether I might be taken away by a social worker or a doctor. Perhaps they wouldn't believe me, and I'd get into trouble with the head-teacher. Yes, that seemed the most likely scenario. Three weeks of detention for causing a fuss. This would be classed as my fault, just like everything else. In English, on Friday, the same teacher was waiting with our essays piled ominously on her desk.

"Well, I have to say I was very impressed with some of your efforts," she said. "And a special mention must go to Patricia King. It was extremely well written, it really was. You got your first A grade, Patricia, so well done."

For a split-second, I was overjoyed. I'd never had higher than a D in an English essay before, so this was quite incredible. There was a slight delay as I processed her comments:

'It was extremely well-written, it really was.'

She had said nothing about the subject matter. Nothing. She hadn't believed me. She hadn't thought it was real. She hadn't even considered the content to be slightly unusual or disturbing in any way.

"Let's see your Grade A essay, Trish," said one of the girls on the desk in front, holding out her hand. I gave it to her, still slightly stunned, and to my horror, she began reading out loud.

'I did my best to hurry past his bedroom door, but I never once got away,' she read. 'I had to get into his bed. I didn't know what he was doing. I just knew...'

An awkward hush fell on the group.

"Oh, this is really sad," she stammered, passing my essay back to me. "Sorry, I didn't realise."

With my head down, I stared at the page, my eyes blurring with tears. I could just make out the big, shouty, A on the front. My first and last A grade, and oh, how I had paid the price for that.

* * * *

Of all the scenarios I had imagined, after submitting my essay, I had not once considered I might simply be completely ignored. Nobody asked me about it. Nobody was in the least bit curious why I had chosen to write so graphically about sexual abuse. There was no referral to the police, to a support worker or a counsellor. They didn't even call home to tell my family.

The indifference, the total absence of interest or concern, was absolutely crushing. I had often tormented myself that I didn't matter, that nobody really cared about me. And this was confirmation that I had been right all along. The disinterest, the disregard, was the worst possible reaction and I felt myself sinking lower and lower. I had been kicked to the kerb like an unwanted dog; just like my poor Tyson.

No wonder nobody likes you Tricia.

My medication continued to pile up on the shelf, and again, nobody noticed or commented. I'd had no fits, which was further proof, in my mind, that I had spent years taking medication I didn't need, enduring horrible side-effects which were totally unnecessary, and attending countless hospital appointments I didn't require, all because no-one challenged my father and his twisted version of events. Nobody thought my home life warranted further investigation.

"You could swallow these tablets, all of them, and it would be over," insisted the voice in my head. "Take them to the railway line and kill yourself. You won't be missed."

It was a dispassionate voice; direct and self-assured. Heavily, I sank to my knees, right there in the kitchen, and I sobbed. I had never felt so desolate or so scared; my life was unravelling, yet again, and this time I had nobody to turn to. I squeezed my eyes closed and wished, helplessly, for a glimpse of the ghost lady. As the tears ran in little rivulets down my face, I longed to feel that warm nose nuzzling my cheek.

"Tyson," I mumbled, remembering the feeling of his warm body close to mine. "Where did you go?"

Over and over, Tyson had saved me. Over and over, he had shown himself to be more loyal, and more devoted than any human being I knew. Now, I had to make my own way in the world, and it was so lonely.

With my essay swallowed up and forgotten in the hum-drum routine of school life, I began to feel more and more alienated. Partially, I disassociated myself from school. In part, perhaps, my school pushed me out. Or rather, I was allowed to simply fall away.

Deeply troubled and disillusioned, I began skipping school more and more. Penny wasn't keen to miss too many lessons, so I started playing truant on my own. I didn't enjoy it so much, of course. But the isolation somehow suited me too.

I was used to it. One afternoon, I was leaning on a wall, waiting for the teenage boys I usually met. There was no sign of them, and instead, I spotted two men, one was on a bike, the other was walking.

"Why isn't a gorgeous girl like you in school?" asked the first one.

I eyed them both suspiciously. They were far older than the boys I usually hung around with, yet they didn't really look like undercover cops or social workers. They were both scruffy and smelled strongly of cigarettes. The idea of undercover cops springing an arrest on me made me giggle a little, awkwardly.

"Don't you get bored just hanging round the precinct?" asked the second one. "I've seen you here before."

"Yeah," I replied. "I do, actually."

The first man, wiry, dark haired and with a heavy stubble, smiled, as he rode slowly round and round me on his bike. I was like a little mouse, with a big cat circling, preparing to pounce. I knew that, yet somehow the element of danger was all part of the appeal. It was just a game, after all.

"How old are you?" he asked.

"Nearly 15," I lied, thinking it sounded more respectable. "What about you?"

"Nearly 40," he said, but I suspected that was a lie too, for entirely different reasons. He looked ancient to me.

"Listen, do you fancy coming back to our place?" he said. "We've got some booze in, we could get a takeaway, listen to music? Better than hanging round here. You shouldn't be out on your own, a young girl like you."

I agreed instantly. He was right; it was a better alternative to what I was doing, and I didn't think about anything further than that. The fact that I was a mouse, being offered sanctuary by a big cat, didn't strike me as in any way contradictory or alarming. Or more likely, it did, and I just ignored the warnings.

"Lead the way," I grinned.

Their house was in Longsight, Manchester, and for a while, I stood in the back yard with the first man, on his bike. The second man, who seemed quite surly, went inside.

"Come on then," he said, throwing his bike down onto the ground. "I'd say we're ready for you now."

Inside, the house was dirty and sparsely furnished. There was no light bulb in the kitchen, and it was gloomy, with a stagnant smell. I had a bottle of blue vodka Wicked thrust into my hand as I was guided into the hallway and then into a dingy downstairs bedroom. There was damp crawling down the wall, patches of black, like small armies of spiders. It was only when I looked from the double bed to the craggy, middle-aged face of the man that I snapped to my senses.

"Look, I need to get home," I stammered. "My mum's expecting me. She'll be wondering where I am."

The man curled his lip and grabbed my sleeve. His fingers were stubby, and nicotine stained. I thought about my father's fingers with the same yellow tips and a shudder ran right through me. This man was old enough to be my father which explained why I needed to escape, and probably also explained why I was here in the first place.

"So how're you gonna pay for that?" he asked, jerking his

chin at the bottle of vodka. His grip on my sleeve tightened and I was suddenly alert with panic. I had about 70p in my pocket, and I needed it for bus fare.

"You can have everything I've got," I said, showing him my loose change. "I'll walk home. I don't care. I just need to go, please. My brothers will be out looking for me."

I didn't think the Kings' reputation for fighting would travel as far as Longsight and, though my mind was racing, I couldn't think of anything convincing to add. I could tell his temper was fraying fast, and then, more out of self-pity than self-preservation, I blurted out:

"I told a lie. I'm only 13 years old. I'm sorry."

He swore and bundled me to the back door. He shoved me out and I landed in his yard, on top of his pushbike, tearing a long scratch down my leg, but at least I was out of there. I ran on jelly legs, all the way to the bus stop.

My heart was pounding as I waited for my bus. I paced up and down, checking the street, in case he came after me. Yet, as the hours passed, my thought processes followed the same cycle as they had with the police. This time, it didn't take as long. On the bus, I was shaken, furious with myself, and vowing never to put myself in danger again. But by the time my stop came, the whole incident had become nothing more than a funny anecdote; something to boast about to all the girls at school, the next day.

'He gave me a bottle of blue Wicked and promised me a takeaway…'

Besides, I had escaped once. So what was to stop me doing it again? I didn't consider I was putting myself in danger, and anyway, I didn't really care. Nobody else bothered about me, so why should I? But that night, I dreamed of the nicotine-stained fingers, reaching for me, grabbing at my sleeve, stroking my face. I woke in a state of cold confusion, my mind thick with fear. I was too restless to go back to sleep and when my alarm went off, I was exhausted. Lisa tapped on the back door the following morning, ready in her neatly pressed uniform with her packed lunch in her bag.

"You ready for school, Trish?" she asked. "You skipped yesterday, so I thought I'd call round. You should go in today."

I shook my head. I didn't know how to explain it to her. I couldn't possibly put my uniform on and sit in class. It was a pretence I could no longer keep up. I had never felt so far away; from school, from Lisa, from myself.

"I'm not well," I told her flatly, and I closed the door.

Still in my pyjamas, I sat and stared at the pile of epilepsy tablets on the archway shelf. My pretty new bob had lost its shape and I needed another trim. But my brother and Claire had split up and he had a new girlfriend now; one who barely glanced in my direction. My hair was limp and straggly again, and I had lost my bounce. Oh, I had certainly lost my bounce.

With my arms wrapped around my chest, I imagined I was whirling down and down, sucked into a plughole, through the drains, spat out into the sewers. The new Trish was slowly disintegrating. The old Tricia had gone, months ago. And so what was left? Who exactly was I now and where did I fit in?

I had no grasp on my own identity, on my own sense of self, and it frightened me. This new rebellion, this brave new me, was not, after all, a burst of confidence or self-assurance, as I had at first tried to convince myself. I realised it was instead symptomatic of a gaping lack of self-belief and self-love. My defiant behaviour was nothing more than a futile attempt to cover up the chasm of pain and sadness and fear which ached and ached inside me.

I looked at the shelf, at the medication which waited for me. It beckoned me over and whispered my name. Again, I wondered if the answer lay inside the layers and layers of blister packs. Again, I just wanted it all to be over.

20

"Let Me Out!"

Drinking blue Wicked and eating cheap burgers became the backdrop to my dark teenage years. I turned 14 and soon after, a boy in my class asked me out on a date. I tried not to appear too flattered or enthusiastic, but deep down, like any girl my age, I was thrilled to have a real boyfriend. If nothing else, it was confirmation that at last I was leaving behind my reputation as the kid with the head lice and the smelly clothes. His name was Ryan, he had a piercing in one ear and a dazzling smile.

"Do you fancy going to the skate park after school?" he asked.

It was hardly the most romantic date, but I was pleased, nonetheless. We spent a few weeks hanging around the park and local shops, and then he invited me home to meet his family.

"My dad asked if you want to come round for tea," he said.

"Let Me Out!"

I knew I was on a sort of trial, and I scrubbed my trainers and wore a dress, which Lisa had given me. Ryan's dad, his grandparents, his brother and sister and even his snowy white cat were all there to meet me. It could have been nerve-racking and excruciating, but they were all so nice. The problem was, I felt far from nice myself. I felt like a complete fraud as we ate chicken and chips around the table and Ryan's gran asked me what subjects I preferred at school.

"They really liked you," Ryan told me later. "I've got the green light to take you round now, whilst my dad's at work. You know…"

He trailed off, too shy to come out with what he was really thinking. Ryan's dad worked long hours as a delivery driver, and his siblings were much older, so we often had the house to ourselves, late in the afternoon. Left to our own devices, our relationship progressed, and early one evening, in the dining room, we decided to go all the way.

"You sure you're OK with this?" Ryan asked, and I nodded.

I had told him, truthfully, this was my first time, and he said it was his too. I didn't for a minute equate what Dad had put me through with what Ryan and I were about to do. It didn't even enter my thoughts. But, after we took off our clothes, and started kissing, I closed my eyes and saw a reel of splintered images, the sunken eyes, the flabby arm, the bloated neck, the pink bedspread.

Inwardly, I recoiled. I tried to push them out, to tell myself that it was in the past. But I had a hot, fuzzy feeling at the back of my eyes. I saw colours, dancing and fragmenting at the edge of my vision. And then, the room closed in on me and everything went dark. When I awoke, I was on the carpet, covered with a blanket, and Ryan was crouching over me in concern.

"I think you've had some sort of seizure," he said. "You just started shaking. Shall I call an ambulance? Do you want me to ring your mum?"

"No, I'm alright," I said weakly, staggering to my feet. "I used to have fits when I was little. I've not had one for years. I'll be fine though. I just need a minute."

Already I could feel the onset of a stonking, ice-lolly crunching, headache and I held my face in my hands. Ryan was white-faced; stricken with worry.

"I'm sorry," I added. "It was probably worse for you than me. I'm fine, really."

He made me buttered toast and a cup of tea, and we sat on the sofa until the headache eased and I started to feel more like my usual self.

"Look, don't worry about it," Ryan said. "Forget the sex. It's just really bad timing. We can try again another day. You should probably get home, see the doctor maybe. I'll walk you back."

I nodded. I couldn't begin to tell him this was no coincidence at all. This was my first seizure since the end of the sexual abuse, and as Ryan and I were having sex, the smells and the sounds had overwhelmed me, like a tidal wave splashing right over my head and knocking my feet from under me. Suddenly, I was seven years old again, my mouth stretched wide into a silent scream as I stared at the colours in the stained-glass door.

****

Having a boyfriend at school did not stop me playing truant and hanging around with older teenagers. It wasn't that I didn't like Ryan; it was probably more because I did like him that my two lives ran parallel and mutually exclusively. He had no idea about my other life, and I wanted to keep it that way; I didn't want to hurt or disappoint him, and I certainly didn't want him caught up in the same mess as me.

Ryan was kind and gentle; he was everything I needed but thought I didn't deserve. I was so conflicted about what relationships actually were, and he got caught up in that; he was yet another casualty of my broken childhood.

"Don't worry, Trish," he told me encouragingly. "We can try again when you're feeling better. I don't mind waiting. You know that."

The next time we tried again we were in his bedroom. It seemed to be going well until, in a genuine show of affection, Ryan looped his arm over me. I froze. All the breath left my lungs. In a flash, I was in my father's big bed, pinned under his heavy arm, skewered to the sheet, like a dead butterfly pinned to a collector's board.

"Let me out," I pleaded, gasping like a dying fish. "Let me out!"

Ryan sat up in bed, perplexed.

"What's wrong?" he asked. "Are you having a seizure? What's going on? Don't you fancy me?"

I shook my head in frustration.

"It's not that," I said.

In the absence of any other explanation, I broke down and told Ryan about the abuse in my childhood.

"That's why I had a seizure when we first tried to have sex," I explained. "I had a flashback to the sexual abuse from my dad and it triggered a fit.

"I can't bear to have your arm around me because it reminds me of him. I feel trapped."

It was a big revelation for a young lad to cope with, but Ryan did his best. He was sympathetic and understanding.

"To be honest, it's not a massive surprise," he told me. "I know your dad went to jail for abusing someone years ago. It all kind of makes sense now. I'm really sorry Trish, you've had such a shit time."

I shrugged.

"You should get some help," he suggested. "Why won't you tell the police? Or one of the teachers? I'll come with you."

"No point," I said dully. "I've tried that. Nobody listens."

Though I had no more seizures, intimacy of any kind was always difficult, because every time it brought into sharp focus the horrific memories of the abuse. Patiently, Ryan learned he could not put his arm over me, and he tried to recognise when I was having flashbacks. Somehow our fledgling love affair muddled on, and in many respects, we were just like any other teenage couple. Ryan and I had a scare after having unprotected sex one evening, and my period was due. I went straight to the GP for a pregnancy test which luckily was negative, and I later asked for birth control advice.

"Better safe than sorry," I told Ryan. "We need to be responsible."

Yet that same weekend, I went out to meet boys from MSN behind his back. Some were teenagers, like me, but most were adults. Again and again I found myself in situations where I could have been endangered or even killed. When I should have been at school, I instead found myself in strange flats and houses, knocking back vodka, watching films and picking at cold chips in polystyrene trays. Before things went too far, I told myself I could always find an excuse to wriggle out of the situation and run to the nearest bus stop. I prided myself on it, as though this was a new skill I was perfecting.

"You did it again, Trish," I breathed, as I flopped down onto my seat on the bus journey home.

21

Playground Gossip

Day to day, my behaviour was becoming more unpredictable and erratic. I didn't understand how sometimes, as with
the pregnancy test, I was capable of behaving sensibly and
maturely, yet mostly I was wildly irresponsible and reckless.

At school the next day, I'd laugh about my latest near miss
with the other girls, glad to be a source of entertainment,
pleased my escapades made me more appealing somehow. I
had a little circle gathered around me in the playground as I
recounted the details. The best part for me was the surge in
popularity. The best part for the others was that they were
not me.

Once, I arranged to meet a boy called Jamie, who told
me he was 14, the same age as me. When I arrived at the
shops, where we'd planned to meet up, I saw immediately

he was twice my age. Even worse, through the critical eyes of a 14-year-old, he had greasy hair and a kind of grungy, unwashed, look about him.

"What did you do?" Penny asked me.

"I just turned and ran away," I laughed. "I left him standing there. He messaged me all night, begging me to come back, telling me he was really 23 years old but just wanted to be my friend."

My friends all laughed too.

"Wow, Trish, you're such a dark horse, we'd never have thought you had this in you," they said.

The truth was, I really didn't have it in me. It was all a façade. I was a sham. I was hiding dark secrets now, just as I had done all my life. I laughed and joked and bragged at school. I hung on Ryan's arm at the skatepark. And then I went home and looked at my epilepsy pills and I was gripped by an overwhelming urge to swallow every single tablet I could get my hands on.

* * * *

Around this time, my brother got a job in a leisure centre and one afternoon I popped in to borrow my bus fare. On my way out of the centre, the security guard stopped me to say hello.

"You're Tricia, aren't you?" he asked. "I've seen you here before."

"Trish," I corrected him.

"Well, if you're ever passing and you fancy a cup of tea in my office, just let me know."

By now, I could cut straight through the euphemism. I was used to this type of proposition.

"Yeah," I smiled. "Maybe I will."

His name was Darren, he was in his mid-30's and he was well-built and stocky. A couple of days later, I took him up on his offer, and he showed me his poky little office at the back of the leisure centre.

"We'll have a cup of tea, and then I'll take you on my round," he smiled.

At 14, I thought I knew exactly what I was getting into. I assumed, naively, ridiculously, that I was the one in control. My plan was to go along with him, admiring his office, trailing round with him on his security checks. And then, I would make it work for me.

I was hoping Darren might buy me something, a takeaway maybe. Or he might take me somewhere nice. He was a grown man, he had weekly wages after all. Perhaps, if I was extra nice, I could persuade him to buy me some more lip gloss and a new perfume.

Like my friends, I had long wish-lists of clothes, shoes, makeup and beauty products. Unlike my friends, I had no access at all to money. There was barely enough in my family to pay for necessities, and there was certainly nothing left for luxuries. And so Darren, whilst not exactly a gift-horse, presented an irresistible opportunity for me. I felt a sort of duty too, to my friends at school, to keep them entertained with the next instalment of my chaotic love life.

"Yeah, I'm going to see him tonight, his shift starts at 8pm," I told my classmates.

"Let us know how it goes, Trish," they said. "We want all the juicy gossip."

Looking back, I was not nearly so calculating nor scheming as I liked to think. Yes, I was looking to entertain my classmates. Yes, I wanted someone to buy me gifts. But the real reason I got involved with Darren was a crippling insecurity and a desperation to be loved. I was a child, and I was desperate to be noticed.

I had no idea at all that I was being groomed, and I was a victim of child sexual exploitation. I didn't know that Darren, along with the creeps off MSN, along with the oddball on the bike, along with my own father, were all sexual predators; paedophiles preying on young and vulnerable girls like me. I had grown up with abuse, and it was just another unpleasant part of my life; as commonplace and accepted as doing my homework or going to bed early on a school night. Darren was simply another rung on my downwards ladder. I was falling, and falling fast, yet I was reaching out to the wrong people to help me back up.

Quickly, I fell into a routine of calling in at the leisure centre when he was working. He bought me phone credit and bags of chips and took me for drives during his shift. In return, I let him kiss me. My view of sex and relationships was so badly skewed and damaged, that I really thought this was a good deal. I thought this was how it all worked with grown-ups.

I was enthralled by Darren, because he was older and he seemed so worldly-wise, but I was also more than a little disgusted by him too. There was something inherently creepy about him which I spotted, even as a child, yet regardless, I felt flattered he wanted to see me and spend time with me. It was a strange, toxic blend and one I would never be able to make sense of.

One night, when the centre was closed, Darren took me on a tour of the building to test the lighting. In the basement, near the junction box, where it was deserted, he pulled me towards him and began kissing me. I didn't mind at first, but the kissing quickly got out of hand, and I started feeling clammy and uneasy. I had a familiar tingly feeling as the rash bloomed on my chest and inched up my neck like a spider. The overpowering smell of Darren's body odour mingling with his cheap, sickly aftershave, was all of a sudden too much for me.

"Please," I gasped, bursting into sudden tears. "Please stop. I can't. I just can't."

Darren looked at me in surprise.

"What's the matter?" he asked.

"It's my dad," I sobbed. "My dad sexually abused me. I can't have sex with you. I need to talk to someone. I need some help."

Darren let me cry on his shoulder for a few moments, and when I stood back, there were unsightly smears of my make-up on his shiny black uniform.

"You'll be fine," he said, pulling me to him and trying to kiss me again.

I did not appreciate at all the sick irony of the situation. Of him blatantly abusing an abused child. Of him taking advantage of me at my very lowest. I had turned to him for help, and instead he was heaping more trauma onto me.

"I need to go," I wept. "My family will be wondering where I am."

Darren kissed me goodbye, and I knew then, though I didn't say it, I wouldn't ever see him again. I had no idea why I'd confided in him; I didn't even really like him. But my mind was frothing with secrets. They were bubbling over, like hot lava, and I couldn't, wouldn't, push them back inside. I had tried telling a teacher and that had failed miserably. So this time, I decided I would tell social services.

22

The Letter

We had a social worker who came to our house, every now and again, and I remembered speaking to a social worker after Dad was jailed. Maybe these were the people who could help me. That night, as soon as I got home, I wrote a letter, two pages of A4, detailing the sexual abuse I had suffered, including the attacks in the bedroom, in the mornings.

"I kept thinking about what had just happened. I was confused," I wrote. "The next day he called me in again and started touching me and told me to get undressed...some of the time he used to make me suck his penis....I was scared. I would try to sneak past his bedroom in the morning...I thought I'd escaped but he'd call my name and tell me to come back to him.'

When the letter was finished, I felt drained, exhausted as if I'd just finished double PE. But I had a strong conviction also that I was doing the right thing. It was a few weeks before the social worker was due to visit. On the day of her arrival, I reread my letter, with a thumping heartbeat, and sealed it in an envelope.

"Here," I said, thrusting it into her hands as she walked through the front door. "Please read it."

I hurried past her, out of the house, not wanting to be around for the inevitable fall-out. When I got home, later, I imagined there would be police waiting, social workers, family members, all sick with horror and regret. And possibly with recrimination too, if I was to be blamed for it, as was the pattern.

As I rounded the corner to our street, I saw there was nobody parked outside. No police car. There was no welcoming party, and as I pushed open the front door, the house was quiet. Everyone was either out or in bed. Bewildered, I waited the next day, and the next, for a major development. But, as with the school essay, there was nothing. I was completely ignored.

* * * *

After I turned 15, in year 10 of high school, I grew sick of hanging around shops and grubby flats. It all seemed so unsophisticated, and it was boring too. Along with another girl from school, who seemed to know all about the local nightlife, I began going to night-clubs.

As I queued in the biting cold for my first ever night-club experience, I was struck too late by the realisation I wasn't nearly old enough and I didn't have any money either.

"How are we going to get in?" I asked my friend, Kelly. "I haven't a penny on me."

"It'll be fine," she told me with a wink. "The bouncers here are very, you know, flexible."

I didn't know what she meant at all, until we got to the front of the queue. One of the bouncers took me round the side of the building, and, in exchange for lifting my dress and allowing him to grope me, I was given free entry to the club. It was a shock, but it was over so fast, before I had a chance to object or even process what had happened to me. Inside the club, we got lots of wanted free drinks and unwanted male attention.

Again, I thought I was the one in control. I really felt as though this was the perfect arrangement. I was getting exactly what I wanted, after all, which was a free night out with free drinks. It didn't once occur to me that I was the victim here, that I had in fact been the victim all my life and this simply was the continuation of many years of devastating exploitation. I have often wondered, looking back, whether an abused child is somehow easily spotted by other abusers, as though I had been in some way branded by those early years of attacks by my father. Did I have it invisibly tattooed on my forehead?

Just as I had been identified as needy by my teachers; a musty waft from my clothes, an unmistakable scent of vulnerability, I was now singled out as easy prey by my predators. The damage by my father was like a barcode, signalling to all other paedophiles that I was troubled and brittle, and I did not have a support network to protect me. How did they know? How did they know I was an easy target? The issue confounded me then and it continues to do so today. For many years, I blamed myself, because I placed myself in dangerous and risky situations, time and time again. But it was more than that; I was fair game, it was a done deal to the men I met.

Was it a sort of prescient paedophilia? In the same way that I could forecast moods or seizures, could they identify vulnerable children, like child-catchers in fairy tales, or like bogeymen in nursery rhymes? I didn't know what it was; a scent, a mood, a pattern of behaviour... And I certainly didn't know how to put it right. Aged 15, however, none of this concerned me.

I met a different man nearly every weekend and I quickly became shockingly promiscuous. One night, I had sex down an alley. Another time, I did it in a graveyard. I had no idea what the men were called and neither did I want to know. Countless nights, I went back to a strange house, to have sex, before making my way home before morning. I never spent the night, because I could not bear to be pinned down in a bed by a big arm. In my childish logic, if I avoided the arm, I was safe. I never thought about the consequences of sleeping around; I never even considered contraception.

My approach to my relationship with Ryan was completely different to my attitude to these men. Instead, I used sex and the risks it brought to divert my thoughts away from the skull-crushing problems inside my head. I didn't want to dwell on the trauma from my childhood and so instead I jammed my head with thoughts of strange men and strange sex. I hoped the more I had sex, the less meaningful it would become, and it would eventually lose its sick association with my father. Part of me met the men in defiance, in rebellion. Part of it was sheer desperation. But the bigger part of me was looking for warmth and happiness.

As a child, I mistakenly linked sex with love and affection; more than anything, I wanted so very much to be loved. But sleeping around inevitably had the opposite effect and the more sex I had, the more I was exploited, the emptier I felt. I had no discernible feelings save the deeply buried and squalid layers of shame, guilt and disgust which ran through my bone marrow. Yet even these were perversely addictive, and I went out, night after night, grinding those layers in deeper still, searching for a mythical solace and comfort I knew I would never find.

"I'm worried about you," Lisa told me. "You're hardly ever at school. You're always hungover. You need to slow down, Trish."

But I didn't know how. I continued putting myself in danger because I felt that was all I was worth. One night, an angry girl chased me out of a nightclub, after getting me mixed up with someone else. I had no idea why she was so annoyed. Fearing I was about to be attacked by her and her friends, I jumped into the first car I saw on the street outside.

"Can you take me home?" I asked the driver, breathlessly.

He was a middle-aged man, on his own.

"I'm not a taxi, you know," he grumbled.

"I know, I'm sorry," I stuttered. "It's just, I'm in a bit of bother."

The Letter

Amazingly, he drove me home, he made sure I got in safely, and he refused to take a penny from me. I was stunned that someone would do me a favour and expect nothing in return. It contradicted everything I had learned so far. When I thanked him, he turned to me, wearily, and said:

"You might not be so lucky next time, love. Have a think about that."

But my crazy night outs continued, and though I never touched drugs, I drank heavily, and I had sex with lots of different men.

My relationship with Ryan ended; it seemed childish and inadequate somehow, and even as I spiralled, I could see it was unfair on him. His days revolved around school, his evenings around the skatepark. My own life was wildly out of control, and I had outgrown him, just as I had outgrown myself. I was on a path of self-destruction, and the more I could hurt myself, the better I felt.

* * * *

Still aged 15, I was hanging around our local shops early one evening when a car with two men inside slowed and stopped to talk to me. I vaguely recognised one of the blokes because he had a girlfriend who lived in our estate. They were both middle-aged, neither of them particularly good-looking or charismatic in any way. But, I reminded myself, they had a car, and jobs, and no doubt more money than I did. Again, I thought I was clever and streetwise; again, I thought I was taking them for fools.

"Get in," said the passenger. "We'll go for a drive."

They told me their names were Andy and Dave. Andy was driving, and I sat in the back with Dave. When we pulled over, Dave nipped into an off-licence and came out with bottles of brightly coloured alcopops and bags of crisps.

"Here, help yourself," he smiled.

Like any teenager, I appreciated the treats, especially the alcohol. But for me, it was more about someone giving me a gift and caring enough to spend money on me. This was proof, in my mind, that they liked me. Following previous patterns, I didn't see them as predators or groomers, or even as threatening in any way. This was, in fact, another glittering opportunity for me. I swapped numbers with both men and over the next few days, they sent me flirty messages.

'Can't wait to see you again.'

'You looked so nice the other night'

'Can't stop thinking about you.'

I didn't find either man remotely attractive. But I was a child, looking for affection and belonging, looking for escape and excitement, and I kidded myself into believing they might be able to offer it.

Neither the legality nor the morality of the situation occurred to me at all, and it didn't seem to bother the two men either. I had grown up believing men and sex were inextricably linked, more, that they were effectively one and the same thing. The fact I was 15 and they were more than twice my age was not a worry for me. I arranged to meet up with Dave and Andy that weekend, and they collected me outside the shops on the estate.

"Quick, get in," Andy hissed. "We don't want people seeing you. They'll all get jealous."

Naively, I jumped into the back seat, thinking how lucky it was they had chosen me. Dave and I kissed on the back seat and then he said:

"How old are you, Trish?"

"15," I replied truthfully. "I turn 16 in November."

"Well, we can't break the law," Dave said, in a responsible voice. "We'll wait till you're 16 before we have sex. We need to do the right thing by you."

I nodded, and he began kissing me again. The hypocrisy washed right over me; I was used to it, after all. Dave spent the next few weeks messaging, discussing his plans for my 16th birthday.

'Can't wait,' he wrote.

'Me neither,' I lied.

I didn't want to sleep with him at all but would never have dared tell him that. I didn't think I had a choice. I could only hope that something would happen, to help me get out of it, at the last minute. And incredibly, my prayers were answered.

That October, as Dave was counting down to having sex with me, his girlfriend found out he was being unfaithful. Luckily, she had no idea I was involved but someone had told her he had been seen kissing a teenage girl in the back of his car. He was chased from the estate by her family and fortunately for me, was too scared to come back. Again, I'd had another narrow escape which served only to convince me that I had an uncanny invincibility when it came to men and sex.

With Andy and Dave out of the picture, I focussed on meeting men online, putting myself at further risk, and not caring at all. I got a part-time job in Greggs bakery and used my wages to buy short skirts, high heels and make-up. I thought I was the envy of all the girls at school, they were full of compliments and seemed envious and impressed when I told stories of my nights out and my boyfriends. Yet none of them wanted to join me. They loved hearing my stories. But that was as far as it went.

23

Doomed To Fail

In September 2003, I began my final year at high school. My attendance had been patchy at best for years 9 and 10, and I assumed the teachers had more or less given up on me. I wasn't punished for skipping school, but neither do I remember being offered support or encouragement to turn it around.

Unofficially, I was a lost cause. Because this was our exam year, there was a noticeable change in attitude amongst many of the kids in my class. Some got home tutors. Others attended intervention sessions. Nobody wanted to hang around the skate park or the shops on the way home from school.

"Sorry Trish, I've got too much homework," Lisa told me. "I need to catch up."

Penny was the same.

"I need good GCSE grades to get into college," she said.

"I'll have to stop messing around. You should think about it too, you know."

I shrugged indifferently.

"Who cares?" I replied.

The following Monday morning, the girls clustered around me in the playground to hear what I'd been up to at the weekend.

"Did you go clubbing?" they asked. "Did you pull anyone? Spill the details, Trish."

They were like flies buzzing around me. Lisa caught my eye, and in her face, I saw a sadness and a resignation that pulled at my heartstrings. In that moment, I felt a dull realisation, like a stone plopping to the bottom of my stomach and settling there. These girls were not my friends. They were not on my side. They didn't care about me at all. Deep down, I'd probably known it all along, but it hadn't seemed to matter too much before. I was nothing more than a source of gossip and amusement to them and they probably talked about me far more than they talked to me.

"See what I mean?" Lisa said afterwards. "You should be thinking about yourself, Trish. You need to start working at school. Give the clubbing a rest, just for a few months."

I sighed.

"Look, try it for a month," she suggested. "If it doesn't work out, you can go back to sagging school."

I agreed. I was in such a mess, and what harm could it do? For my options, I was studying textiles and child development and in those first few weeks, the teachers announced projects in each subject, which would form part of the final grade. As I got started with my plans, I really began enjoying my work. My grades were at rock bottom, but slowly, they began to climb. The trial month passed, and I said to Lisa:

"You were right. I'm going to give it my best shot this year."

I still went out at weekends, drinking and clubbing; I couldn't give it up completely. The promise of human warmth, the offer of affection and love, even if it was a false one, was too tempting to resist. Drinking was an escape for me; an anaesthetic. A way of temporarily shutting out my reality. But despite my nights out, my school attendance was improving, and I made more of an effort in class. I didn't want to admit it, but I was actually really enjoying my school-work. All too soon it was May, and the GCSEs began. After sitting each paper, I was engulfed with regret and remorse. I knew, if I'd applied myself sooner, I could have performed well. As it was, I'd done too little, too late.

"Don't worry, Trish," Lisa said. "You did your best."

At our leaving ceremony, I was awarded the prize for: 'Most Improved Student.' As my name was read out, in the final assembly, I felt a swell of pride, but annoyance too. My teachers had noticed me, they had cared, to a degree at least. The gesture touched my heart, but it seemed they, like me, just did not care quite enough.

I left school that summer and later learned I'd failed most of my exams, with passes only in Science, Child development and Textiles. It was what I expected, yet the failure left a bitter taste, just the same. I enrolled at college to study health and social care, which I enjoyed and was determined to work hard at. I started seeing a new boyfriend too, named

Callum, who was my own age. The situation at home was still difficult and there was very little money. Now I was almost 17, I was informed I was expected to provide for myself and also contribute to the running of the house.

"That's just not possible on my wages," I sighed. "I only work on Saturdays."

I quickly realised I needed a full-time wage and by Christmas, I'd had to leave my college course and I was working full time at Greggs. The irony was, after years of avoiding my studies, I really missed them now.

* * * *

With a regular wage, I worked out I could soon save enough money to move out and get my own place.

"Do you fancy getting a place together?" I asked Callum.

"Why not?" he agreed.

He and I weren't really serious, but moving in together suited us both. I found a new job, in insurance, which paid more. In what I felt was an uncharacteristic display of maturity, I applied for a sexual health test online, realising my new start with Callum had to spell the end of my promiscuity. I wanted to put it behind me now; I felt it was time to grow up. I completed the test and returned the swab by post, and soon forgot all about it. But several days later, I got a text message to say I'd tested positive for chlamydia and needed to see my GP for antibiotics.

Sitting in the surgery, I was mortified, as any girl my age would be, but I was also realistic and knew I had probably escaped very lightly. The fact I was still alive was something of an achievement in itself, given my reckless lifestyle and my lists of near misses.

Callum and I rented a crummy flat, near on the outskirts of Manchester city centre, and again, it felt like a new chapter as we signed our tenancy agreement and paid a deposit. Packing my belongings, in my old bedroom, I felt strangely numb. Even though I had lived here all of my life, I felt no connection here. There was no nostalgia or fondness. Certainly no regret at leaving. I took one last look around the room and I saw Tyson's ghostly image bounding in through the door, laying his head on my pillow, offering me his comforting white paw. I missed him, I missed all my animals. But I kept those memories in my heart, not in this house.

"Miss you, Ty," I murmured.

With my case zipped up, I dragged it across the landing, and paused at my father's bedroom door. In my mind's eye, I saw my six-year-old self, scurrying, scared witless, across the carpet, terrified of hearing him clear this throat and call my name. I remembered his big hand and yellow fingers patting the bed; the non-verbal command for me to climb up next to him. I felt again the raw panic as my Care Bear pyjamas were pulled down below my knees. Even now, I felt so exposed, so vulnerable, so afraid. Downstairs, as I passed the living room, I could not allow myself to look at the stained-glass door. I could not let that memory loose. I knew I wasn't strong enough.

"You're out of here," I reminded myself firmly. "Just forget about all this. You can leave it all in the past."

Yet strangely, instead of the whoosh of relief I'd expected as the front door slammed behind me, I felt a gnawing sense of guilt. There was no rational explanation for it; whatever I did, I just felt I was in the wrong. It was my fault I was leaving, just as it was my fault I had been abused. I thought it would be a new start with Callum, and for the first couple of weeks, we had fun. But the cracks showed soon enough.

We were both so young and hardly knew each other and besides, I had no idea of how real partnerships worked. In some ways, I was grown-up and world-weary; I was able to clean, cook and shop. I knew how to work the washing machine; I knew how to budget. Moving out of home did not offer a new taste of independence, in the way it does for most teenagers, because I had already had my fill of nights out and one-night stands. I had overdosed on freedom so many times that now the feeling was turning rather stale. Emotionally though, I was still very immature and insecure. I purposely picked arguments with Callum, as a perverse way of proving what I meant to him. I plucked out bizarre examples; each designed to prove my worth, each looking to seal my value as a person.

"If you go out with your friends tonight, then you don't love me," I told him defiantly. "I mean it. We're finished if you don't stay at home."

We had so many silly, circular arguments, aggravating and fuelling each other. Underneath it all, my hyper-vigilance reared yet again, and all of my interactions, at home, at work, socially, were dominated by my anxiety. If I was having a conversation with Callum, or maybe chatting with a colleague at work, I was so busy examining their face for signs of dislike, that I barely heard their words.

I was worried nobody liked me, I was worried nobody loved me, and I constantly looked for minuscule signs in body language which proved my point. I analysed every word Callum and I exchanged, until I was exhausted by it. Our relationship was simultaneously demanding and intense, yet ridiculously silly and juvenile.

"If you don't find the TV remote, then you don't love me." I'd tell him. "I'm serious. I'm moving out if you don't help me look for it."

Every weekend, I drank too much and many times I put my own safety at risk. Though I had stopped sleeping around, I was still sinking in a downward spiral of emotional self-harm. Once, after a night of partying, I passed out on a bench in a city centre park. I was woken in the early hours by a homeless man who was complaining I was on his own personal bench.

"I sleep here because I've nowhere else to go," he told me. "What's your excuse?"

"Don't know," I shrugged, bleary-eyed.

It should have been a bright red flag for me, but I just staggered back to the flat, and went out drinking again the following weekend. My favourite part of the week was Sunday lunch with Callum's family; I loved turning up with a bottle of wine or a chocolate cake. Callum's mum was busy at the stove, straining carrots or stirring gravy. There was football on the telly and his family all gathered round, squashing up on the sofa, jostling for room.

This was what I craved; normality. I wanted so much to be accepted into the bosom of a family and loved. If not my own family, then I would hop into someone else's, like a cuckoo, and hope they wouldn't mind. But though I loved his family, my relationship with Callum had been doomed to fail, right from the start.

24

Beginnings And Endings

As the months passed, it became increasingly toxic and dysfunctional. Having my own place, on my own terms, was nothing like I had imagined, and it confused and depressed me even more. I wanted so much to leave my childhood behind. I wanted to be normal; whatever that was. But I didn't know how. I didn't know where I was going wrong. And the memories of the abuse, much as I tried to squash them into a forgotten corner, squatted in my stomach like a tumour. They lurked in the shadows of my mind, and I could not erase them.

I had carried the poisons from my family home with me into my flat; they had leaked through my skin and left a stain on my soul. I was the problem, not the building. I had moved away from the pink bedroom, from the stained-glass window, from the shed where my pets had been killed. But I could not move away from myself. Helplessly, hopelessly, my mind swung around, more than once, to the piles of medication on the old archway shelf at home.

My epilepsy drugs were long gone. I hadn't had a seizure since the one at Ryan's house, aged 14. But often, especially when I was drunk, I tried to pluck up courage to slit my wrists or overdose on the contents of the medicine cupboard. In my darkest moments, I made sketchy, ill-conceived plans to end my life, but in the end, I could never go through with them. My over-riding fear was not of dying, but of getting it wrong; of messing up my suicide attempt and getting into trouble for it.

'You make a mess of everything, Tricia! You're useless. No wonder nobody likes you.'

At night, I was tormented by recurring nightmares. I found myself trapped in an underground carpark, where I was being chased by something I couldn't quite see. For a few minutes, I hid in a store cupboard, and shivered as I saw a dark shape slithering past. Out of the cupboard, I ran up a flight of concrete steps, into a kitchen, towards a front door.

All around me there was paper and litter spookily swirling, as if I was in the middle of a storm. I knew the front door was my route to freedom, but as I reached out, and I saw my fingers stretching to touch the handle, I woke up. It happened again and again, and during every dream, I awoke just before I reached the door handle. I was shivering, sweating, sobbing. Sometimes, the bed was soaked with sweat, and I had to wake Callum so I could change the sheets.

"Sorry," I mumbled, as he rolled out of bed, and I stripped the sheets. "Bad dreams."

I'd not heard any news from Dad since that phone call just as he was jailed. It was not so much that I missed him. Now that I was growing up, I didn't think of him as often, but still, sometimes, I wondered about what might have been. I hankered after something I would never have. I had no idea where he was living or what he was doing. And yet, his abuse dominated my life; awake and asleep.

In my nightmare, I never knew whether I got out of the door safely. Deep down, I couldn't help worrying that I probably didn't. The nightmares were raw and immediate, and the worst thing was, they were my reality, too. I would never, ever, feel safe. Callum eventually suggested I should see my GP.

"Maybe you're right," I conceded.

I knew there was no physical cause for my bad dreams, and I asked the doctor, instead, if I could be referred to a counsellor. Aged 18, I booked in for my first counselling session, and on my way to the appointment, on the bus, I rehearsed what I might say to her. I planned to include my excess drinking, the incident of me falling asleep on the park bench, and my self-destructive streak which seemed to threaten all my relationships. I had a definite plan in place. When I arrived, the counsellor asked:

"So, Patricia, what brings you here?"

To my amazement, I heard a brutally honest account, rushing and tumbling from my mouth, as if a seam had been ripped open. I had not anticipated this at all. I told her about the sexual abuse from my father, the deaths of my pets, the bailiffs, and my reckless early teenage years sleeping around. It felt to me as though I barely paused for breath throughout the whole session.

"I didn't intend to tell you any of this," I admitted. "I don't know what came over me."

The counsellor suggested I should report the sexual abuse to the police.

"Yes," I agreed. "I'll do that. You're right."

I left the appointment feeling light and euphoric. The journey home hardly registered; I was literally floating on a cloud. Just sharing my burden was like having a concrete slab lifted off my chest. I had another session booked in with the counsellor and I couldn't wait.

Over the next few days, my dreamy, airy thoughts gradually became clouded and muddied and I felt the heavy slab settling back into place on my chest. I realised there was no way I could go to the police. I didn't know what I'd been thinking of. My father would be furious, for a start. How could I be responsible for putting him in prison, when he had expressly told me he was frightened of the place? He had told me himself that it was a genetic fault, and he couldn't help it. *I'm made this way.* How could I land him in trouble for something he could not control? The entire counselling session felt, to me, like a rush of adrenaline, a messy haemorrhage, a huge and idiotic mistake, which I could not repeat.

"That counsellor was a waste of time," I said to Callum. "Not bothering next week."

When my next appointment came around, I ignored it. I blocked the counsellor's number, and never went back. Years later, I would learn the counsellor made a complaint to the police on my behalf, after I missed my second appointment. But her concerns went no further. So, even when a third party intervened, on my behalf, I was ignored and disregarded. My suffering just did not matter at all.

* * * *

After two years together, Callum and I split, and I went to stay with one of my older brothers. I had stayed in touch with one sibling, after leaving home, and he kindly helped me save for a deposit for a new place in Cheadle Hulme, Greater Manchester. I found a new job, in a building society, which paid a little more than my last one.

Since college, I'd been friends with a boy off my course named Simon. I'd known he fancied me from the start; he'd asked me out several times, but I didn't feel the same. Even so, we'd kept in touch after I left the course. Now, after the turmoil and uncertainty of living with Callum, I craved stability and security. I wanted a partner who genuinely cared about me. Simon was uncomplicated, undemanding, and absolutely devoted to me. So this time, when he asked me on a date, I agreed.

Even then, I knew we were both looking for different things and I feel ashamed, looking back, that I took advantage of him. It's not an excuse, but at 19, I was very mixed-up and confused. I had a deep sadness, a void within me, and I was constantly searching for ways to fill it, constantly looking for ways to obliterate the secrets of my past.

For a few months, we were really happy. Simon couldn't do enough for me. I had to be at the bus stop for 5.30am to get to work, and he insisted on getting up early to drive me there. He'd bring me coffee and a bag of my favourite strawberry bon-bons. He even made me a playlist of my favourite tracks, to listen to on the bus, 'Tell Me', by Bobby V, 'Wishlist' from Ray J and, good advice perhaps for Simon and I – Musiq's 'Just friends.' I was touched by his kindness, and surely such devotion could only be a good sign.

Around a year later, we moved down to Birmingham, where Simon's family were based. I found a new job, working in the offices of an examining board. But being in a new environment, where I knew nobody but Simon, made me realise all the more just how badly suited we were. The move forced me to confront what I had been trying to avoid for so long. I felt suffocated and smothered, and I missed Manchester terribly. I knew, as I had always known, Simon and I should have stayed as friends, and nothing more.

"What is wrong with me?" I fretted. "Why can't I just be happy?"

I couldn't live with nasty. I couldn't live with nice. Could I live with anyone at all? I was angry with myself, and disappointed, but I felt I had to be honest.

One Wednesday night, I said to Simon:

"I'm sorry, I'm leaving. I'm going back to Manchester."

He was devastated, as I had predicted. The following morning, I was on a train back north. I had broken Simon's heart, and I didn't feel proud of it then, or now. I hope one day he might forgive me and understand that, though there are no excuses, I did have reasons for my poor behaviour. Penniless, rudderless, homeless, once again, I felt like a leaf on the wind, buffeted from one failed relationship, from one forgettable flat, to the next.

After a day of scrolling through the rental ads, I found a cheap, bug-infested bedsit in Manchester's Northern Quarter. It was poky and grubby, but it was a place of my own and I soon had it cleaned up and looking nice. I found another job in insurance and I threw myself into my work.

Each morning, at 4.30am, I was in the gym. I was at my desk soon after 6am, and I worked until after 6pm. Focussing solely on my career, I really enjoyed being single. I wanted a break from men, and from people full stop. I was fed up with relationships in general.

All my life, I had yearned for approval and inclusion, but this time, I didn't even try to make new friends at work or in the gym. I lived in my own little bubble, pushing myself so hard that I was hopefully too tired to let myself dwell on the past. Pounding the treadmill, with my heart racing, I blotted out the memories. I blotted out myself. Like the drinking, it was a temporary sticking-plaster, not a solution, and I knew that. But it was all I was capable of at the time. And still, the nightmares tormented me.

Night after night, I ran around the car park, feeling the burn in the back of my legs as I raced up the concrete steps. And every time I reached towards the door, every time I was just one step from freedom, I woke up. Sitting up in bed in the middle of the night in the flat on my own, I was confronted by the silence. An aggressive, intrusive, threatening silence. It screeched in my ears, it whistled through my brain, and I hated it.

I lived in my studio flat for six months, before Lisa called to say she'd split up with her boyfriend. She was living on her own in a flat in Withington, Manchester, and invited me to move in with her.

"Say yes," she pleaded. "I've missed you."

"Yes!" I replied. "Course it's a yes! Can't wait!"

I was soon packed up and on my way to another new start. It was just like the old days living with Lisa; she and I giggling together on the sofa, bitching about our ex-partners over pizza and wine.

"It was so much easier chatting up boys on MSN," I laughed. "Remember the boys I used to meet online? God, I was so naïve. I thought I knew all about relationships. Remember how I used to pile on the lip gloss and the mascara and pretend I was five years older than I was? I thought I was so grown up, yet I knew nothing."

Lisa smiled.

"We were all the same at that age," she said. "We all thought we knew it all."

I took a deep breath and twisted my hands together.

"Lisa," I began. "When I talked about relationships and stuff, back then, I didn't tell you the truth. I couldn't do it. But I want to do it now."

In between sobs, I finally shared with her the story of the sexual abuse which had wrecked my childhood. As I spoke,

I was aware of Lisa grasping one of my hands and holding it tightly in hers.

"I always suspected it," she said, her tears flowing faster even than mine. "I never wanted to ask you outright, Trish, but I worried so much about you."

"You were always there for me," I told her. "And that was enough. You'll never know what that means to me."

That night, I dreamed not of the car park but of men, hordes of men, chasing me down endless, dimly lit corridors. I ran faster and faster but still, they were gaining on me, and there were so many of them. My t-shirt was sticking to my back with sweat, and I could almost smell the perspiration, even in my dream. Again, I woke before the chase ended, with the looming fear that I never ever made it to safety.

25

Happiness At Last

In March 2014, feeling I was ready to venture out of my self-imposed bubble, I joined a dating site. Lisa and I scrolled through page after page of possible suitors and wrinkled our noses in dismay.

"Not him, not him, not him," I said. "Oh please. And definitely not him. Him…maybe."

I embarked on several disastrous dates, each one slightly more calamitous than the last. On my first date, as I greeted my mystery man in the street, he leaned in for a full-on snog. I hadn't even introduced myself properly before he lunged in for the kiss and I took a step back and covered my mouth. I didn't even stay for a drink with him and got straight back on the bus home, unsure whether to laugh or cry.

The second date was with a man who at first seemed the perfect gentleman as we ordered drinks in a fancy bar. But he

228

then insisted on calling me 'Twish' all night, because he said he thought it sounded cute.

"Shall we do this again, Twish?" he asked me. "Please, Twish?"

"Oh, I'm not sure," I said politely. "It's been lovely, but I'm just not ready for this commitment."

I made my excuses and rushed to the bus stop. For my third attempt, I wore high waisted fake leather leggings, and met my date, who was in his mid-twenties, in a pub. I noticed, as we chatted, that he was staring, fixedly, at my legs. I was beginning to feel self-conscious, as though there was something wrong with my outfit.

"What is it?" I asked. "Why are you looking at my legs?"

"Oh, I have such a fetish for shiny clothes," he replied conspiratorially. "I do love your leggings."

I spat my drink back into the glass in alarm and left immediately. I couldn't even bring myself to say goodbye. Back at the flat, after spilling the gross details of yet another dreadful date to Lisa, I began to think I might be better off single after all. But one night, I was half-watching the telly and half checking my phone, and I spotted the most gorgeous man on the dating app. He had huge blue eyes.

"Beautiful eyes," I commented, and for some reason, I added: "Honest eyes, too."

Craig Hinde had included in his profile that he liked dogs and walking. I felt myself warming to him more and more. We messaged and arranged to meet at the Frog and Bucket, Manchester's comedy club, later that week. I had such a good feeling about this date, and I made a big effort, wearing a black bodycon dress, with red lipstick. Somehow, in my enthusiasm, I arrived 15 minutes early, and there was no sign of Craig. I ordered us both a drink and then spotted a message on my phone.

'Really sorry, bus was so late,' he wrote. 'I will be there soon.'

Sipping my glass of wine, I waited, with Craig's pint of lager untouched opposite me. The minutes dragged and I caught the security staff looking over and pointing, no doubt taking bets on whether or not I'd been stood up. I ordered myself another drink and oddly, though I'd now been waiting over half an hour, I felt absolutely certain Craig was going to show.

"Honest eyes," I reminded myself. "He won't let me down."

Sure enough, a full 45 minutes after my arrival, Craig fell through the door of the club, filled with apologies.

"Nightmare journey," he said, with a gorgeous smile. "I am so sorry."

We started chatting and I was struck straightaway by how calm and kind Craig was. There was a sort of composure about him; as though nothing rattled him; as though he took everything in his stride. He was completely different to anyone I had ever met and certainly the very antithesis of my own family.

Craig began telling me about his childhood, his lovely siblings and his devoted parents. I made comparisons with the anarchy within my own family home and realised how at odds our lives were. Craig had a good, settled, job in banking. I had moved jobs and homes more often than I dared to admit. And yet, we got on so well. The night flew by and at the end, there were no mind games, no awkward silences. Craig saw me safely home and as we said goodnight, he placed a protective hand on the bottom of my back; nothing more.

"I really would like to see you again," he said.

We arranged to meet a couple of days later for a drink and I could barely wait.

"I've found him at last," I told Lisa. "He's the one. I can just feel it."

By our third date, I could feel myself falling for him. And falling fast, too.

"Craig, I need to tell you something," I said apprehensively.

I felt the old familiar rash sneaking up my neck, betraying my anxiety. Craig listened as I told him all about the abuse from my childhood. I hadn't expected to go into detail, but he asked me lots of questions, and he seemed genuinely moved.

"I'm telling you, because I understand if you don't want to see me again," I said sadly. "I understand if you feel I am too damaged."

Even as the words left my lips, I felt my heart breaking. Why did I have such a low opinion of myself? Why was I always on a mission to ruin things, just as they started to go well? I couldn't help it. But I sensed Craig and I were falling in love, and I felt it best he knew now, rather than later.

Looking back, I think my announcement was a subconscious attempt to sabotage the relationship because I didn't think I deserved to be happy. I definitely didn't think I deserved a man like Craig. But when I had finished speaking, Craig took both my hands and said gently:

"Trish, I'm not walking away. No way. I'm shocked by what you told me. But it makes me admire you. It makes me want to get to know you better."

It was a response I just hadn't expected, and I was speechless. I wasn't used to this at all. In the weeks to come, I met Craig's family, his parents and relatives. He had a loving, stable background. He was offering me everything I did not have and everything I had always dreamed of.

His family welcomed me and grew to love me as though I was one of their own, and I could not express to them how much that meant to me. Craig and I settled into a serious relationship, living temporarily with his mum, Sue, whilst we made plans for our future together. I returned to college to re-sit my GCSE exams and then I got a job as a teaching assistant.

We welcomed two dogs into our lives; a labrador called Autumn and Summer, a cocker spaniel. We had so much to look forward to, so much to be grateful for. All my life, I'd felt I was labouring under a curse, but it was lifting now, like a fog burning away in the sun's warmth, and all I could see ahead was brightness.

* * * *

Craig and I both agreed we'd love to have children and around a year into our relationship, we started trying for a baby. In the autumn of 2015, I missed a period and discovered I was pregnant. We were over the moon. I loved how excited Craig was, just as much as me, and he suggested we start looking to buy our own place, ready for our new arrival.

"I'd like that," I smiled. "Our very own home."

I celebrated my 28th birthday on November 5 and Craig cooked me a romantic meal, at his mum's to celebrate. After we'd eaten, he took me out in the garden and lit one single golden firework. He knew how I hated the bangers and rockets from my childhood and had instead chosen one which showered us with golden sparkles. As I was admiring the firework, I heard Craig nervously saying my name. I turned, to see him down on one knee, with a diamond solitaire engagement ring in his palm.

"I love you so much, Trish," he said. "Please will you marry me?"

I threw myself into his arms.

"Yes!" I yelled. "You know I will! I love you too!"

I'd had so many nights where I did not sleep through fear, sadness, or pain. But that night, sheer joy kept me awake. I was bursting with happiness. This was the kind of dream ending I thought was reserved for other people, and not for me. My life, up to now, had been like a constantly shaking snow globe, with no security, no roots, no forward plan. With Craig, the snowflakes were settling around us, and finally, I felt at peace. Finally, I felt loved.

The first few months of my pregnancy brought me back down to earth, as I was constantly sick and was twice admitted to hospital with hyperemesis gravidarum, or extreme morning sickness. After a few days on a drip, to rehydrate, I was well enough each time to come home. But the sickness persisted, and I was ill so much of the time. And yet, running alongside the nausea, was the glorious knowledge that I was going to be a mum, I was going to have a baby of my very own, and I would never be alone again.

All my life, I'd felt like someone who didn't quite fit in, someone who struggled with relationships and friends. I'd spent so much time on my own. But I no longer needed to worry about that. I had a baby, growing and thriving inside me, dominating every moment, and I loved it. Secretly, I even loved the sickness, because of the joy it signified.

Each time my thoughts drifted towards my father, I reminded myself that I was no longer an isolated little girl. I was an adult, soon to be a parent myself, and the realisation gave me strength.

"I think I've found something to distract you from being sick," Craig announced one evening, showing me a photo on his phone of a lovely house for sale.

"I've made an appointment for us to see it," he continued. "We can afford it. Just."

The house was perfect. It was on a quiet road, in Manchester, just around the corner from Sue. She had become a surrogate mum to me, and I valued her advice and friendship and above all, her love. The new house had a long back garden with a gate leading to a woodland path, into a leafy vale.

"I love it," I said to Craig. "I really do."

Our offer was accepted, and I just couldn't wait. Every day

after work, I'd detour to the road, and just park my car and stare in sheer wonder at the house.

"I'm stalking the house," I admitted to Craig. "I can't help myself."

We got the keys at the end of 2015, and on our first night, we shared a chippy tea as we cuddled up on a cream carpet together.

"These light-coloured carpets won't last long," I giggled, as Autumn and Summer rolled around play-fighting.

I loved our new home, and it was those mundane little pieces, slotting together to form the jigsaw of family life, which I appreciated beyond words. I loved having a full fridge, hot water, carpets and curtains. I enjoyed having monthly direct debits, doing weekly shops, putting the bins out each Wednesday night ready for Thursday morning collection.

It all meant so much to me. I'd never had routine, assurance, and certainty before. I'd never truly been loved. And it was worth the wait. In July 2016, our baby boy, Jacob, was born, six days early after a mammoth 23-hour labour. Craig held my hand through it all. Jacob weighed in at 7lbs 7ozs and had big blue eyes, just like his daddy. The first moment I held him in my arms, I felt a rush of love so powerful it left me dizzy.

"Welcome to the world, baby boy," I murmured.

He had the squishiest cheeks and chubby little thighs and I fell madly in love with him. But as I cradled him, I was struck too by the enormity of what it meant to be a parent, and my thoughts drifted to my dad. As Jacob's tiny fingers furled around mine the magnitude of my own father's unspeakable betrayal hit me with full force. The shock was like having my innards sliced.

I was angry with myself for even allowing memories of my father to taint Jacob's arrival. But I could not help myself. I imagined my father, cuddling me as a new-born, whispering promises, taking proud photographs. Yet by the age of six, he was sexually abusing me. At seven, he forced himself on me. At eight, I had to give him oral sex. Only now, as I held my baby in my arms, did I appreciate and understand the bottomless depth of the deception, the revolting extent of the evil. I felt a surge of confused fury. How had my father gone from doting new dad to child sex offender? How did any human being make that distorted leap? Or had he ever even been a doting new father? Did he look at me, new-born, and see only the possibility of grotesque self-gratification? Was that why he wanted a last child, a youngest daughter, so he could abuse me? I felt sick to my soul.

"Are you OK, Trish?" Craig asked gently. "You look pale. Here, give me the baby, you have a sleep. You've done all the hard work now."

"I'm OK," I mumbled, wiping away my tears. "I just feel overwhelmed by it all."

I was at once ecstatic, bursting with love and elation, and yet also filled with a molten hatred and resentment. How could my own father – the one man entrusted to protect and nurture me - have failed me so catastrophically? Baby Jacob and I were allowed home later that same day and Craig's family rushed to visit, bringing presents for Jacob and me.

Behind my smiles, I felt a pang that my father was not there. I absolutely didn't want him there but at the same time, there was still that feeling of guilt, clawing away at my insides.

I felt I was letting everyone down, Jacob especially, because I could not supply a fussing, doting, grandfather for him. I was lacking. I was falling short. As a mother, as a daughter, I was to blame. Again, somehow, it was my fault.

* * * *

Through my tortured childhood, my lonely teens, my lowest points of suicide and self-loathing, I had been waiting, clinging on, for something. And now, I knew, I had been waiting to become a mother. Life was wonderful and fulfilled and complete; in a way I could never have imagined possible. I celebrated and treasured each small triumph. I took Jacob out each day in his pram, walking in the vale behind our home and beyond. I was so enthusiastic to show him the world, and to show him off to the world too.

When he smiled for the first time, I burst into tears of delight. I could not contain myself, nor could I believe how lucky I was. Sometimes, we took the bus into the city centre, to see Craig on his lunch hour, before riding all the way home again. It was worth it; just for Craig to see his son and for Jacob to see his daddy. Craig was promoted at work, and in early 2017, I discovered I was pregnant again.

We were both thrilled; we wanted the children close together. More than anything, I wanted them to share the sibling bonds I'd never experienced. My second pregnancy was not so fraught, and though I suffered with morning sickness, it was not serious enough to require hospitalisation. That summer, Craig and I decided to get married, secretly, at the Dukinfield Register office. We had no guests, no fuss, no reception. It was exactly how we wanted it.

"Mrs Hinde," he beamed, kissing me on the steps of the register office. "My wife, at last."

The words made me so proud. Our second son, Oscar, was born in October 2017, weighing 6bs 13ozs. He chose to arrive at a moment when the midwife was out of the room making Craig a cup of tea, and so the new dad himself stepped in to welcome his son into the world.

"Baby Ozzy, "I smiled, as I held him. "My beautiful boy. Big blue eyes like your daddy, too."

26

Healing Old Wounds

Jacob was only 16 months old when Oscar was born so I had my hands full. Craig was working full-time, but he was a devoted, hands-on dad nonetheless. He did more than his fair share of changing nappies and bathing and bottle feeds. One evening, soon after Oscar was born, I was busy feeding him on the sofa when Craig took Jacob upstairs for his bath. I heard Craig laughing and cooing and singing nursery rhymes. But then, it was silent, save for the sound of the running water.

"Craig?" I called uncertainly. "What's up?"

"Nothing," he replied cheerfully. "We're waiting for the bath to fill."

Deep inside, I felt a prickle of anxiety, a sharp jolt of mistrust. As quickly as it came, I pushed it out again. But it was impossible to ignore.

"Craig!" I yelled again, more insistently. My heart was hammering now.

"What?" he replied. "What's the matter?"

I choked back the words. I didn't know how to say it out loud. I could not articulate that in my own childhood, whilst the rest of the family was carrying on with day-to-day tasks downstairs, my father had sexually abused me upstairs.

"Craig is not your father," I told myself firmly. "Stop it, Trish. Stop it."

But I couldn't escape it. Having my own children had brought into sharp focus how much my own father had let me down, and how effectively he had conned and brainwashed everyone around him for years. How could I be sure it wouldn't happen again? No matter how much I tried to tell myself this was different, I just didn't like Craig looking after our babies on his own. Not because I had any reason to suspect him; not at all. He was a wonderful, wholesome, committed dad. The problem was with me, not with Craig, yet that did nothing to solve it.

Again and again, I shoved the suspicions out of my head, but each time, they gate-crashed their way back in. In the end, I cut Oscar's feed short and carried him upstairs with me. I found Craig playing peep with Jacob whilst he chuckled and splashed in the bath.

"What on earth's the matter?" Craig asked me. "Are you not feeling well?"

My eyes swam with bewildered tears of shame.

"I'm sorry," I sobbed. "I can't help it. I find it so hard to trust you with the kids. I find it hard to trust anyone at all."

Any other man might have been angry or upset or offended. But Craig put his arm around me and said:

"Look Trish, this is probably perfectly normal, considering what you've been through. Why don't you think about seeing a counsellor? Maybe reporting this to the police?"

I nodded. I knew he was, as always, anchoring me. We both agreed Craig should not do anything different. I did not want to restrict him as a father, or for the boys to be deprived of spending time alone with him. I would learn to manage my paranoia the best I could and seek professional support.

After Jacob's bath, we all climbed on the bed and read Julia Donaldson's 'Zog and the Flying Doctors.' It was our favourite book at the time. Jacob loved the pictures and Craig did a funny voice for every page.

"See," I remonstrated with myself. "See! You're being ridiculous, Trish. Stop it."

For a couple of days, I managed to keep my angst at bay. But then, one night at 3am, Oscar woke up crying and Craig climbed out of bed to feed and change him.

"I'll do it, you get some sleep," he yawned.

The rational side of me was telling me how kind and thoughtful Craig was. But another, louder voice was telling me not to leave Oscar alone with him.

"No, I'll do it," I replied. "Please, just let me do it."

I knew I was being over-protective. I knew I was being unreasonable. But that didn't make me feel any better. In fact, it made me feel worse. The seed was sown, and it grew and spread like a cancer, until it filled my chest, choking me of oxygen, until it felt as though it would rupture and rip me apart.

* * * *

I took Craig's advice and contacted the NSPCC abuse line early in 2018. Over the phone, I told a counsellor about the abuse by my father, and she said:

"Would you like me to report this for you? Or would you like to report it yourself?"

"Can you do it please?" I asked.

It was draining, explaining it all to her and I could not face going through it all again. She promised she would speak to the police and advised me to expect a call.

"You did the right thing, Trish," said the counsellor. "Well done."

The weeks passed, and I was on tenterhooks, expecting a call or a letter from the police. But nothing happened. I accepted, slowly, painfully, that once again, I had been overlooked. This was the fourth time I had tried to report the abuse. This was the fourth time I had been failed. It ought to have been easier to accept, by now. But the feelings of rejection and worthlessness got worse each time, as though they were being ground into my skin, deeper and deeper still.

This felt like a fourth twist of the knife, a fourth slap in the face. Four separate pieces of proof that I did not matter at all. In later years, I would discover the NSPCC had passed my complaint to police, as promised, but it was not, for some reason, followed up. I felt the curse descending upon me again, smothering me with a blanket of shame and guilt. Meanwhile, my suspicions about Craig were like a malignancy; a capillary network of neuroses spreading right through my mind. I didn't like him changing the boys' nappies or bathing them on his own. I had to be present, to supervise, all the time, just to put my mind at rest.

At night, patchy slideshows of reminders whirred round my mind, on repeat. My thoughts were slippery and suffocating; I jumped from one horrific memory to the next, reliving the abuse, again and again, remembering the raw pain and agony. I vowed not to let my children's lives be ruined by my own childhood horror. But I also vowed never to leave them vulnerable to abuse. How could I achieve both? Our children were innocent, angelic and pure and my own paranoia was purposely sullying this purity. I felt so angry with my father for creating such division, such fear. But I felt even angrier with myself.

****

Over the summer of 2018, I fell pregnant again. Though I had all-day morning sickness again, it was not as serious as it had been with Jacob and my days were busy, looking after the boys, running our home, and running to the bathroom. Lisa popped round one morning and asked:

"How's the sickness? Any better?"

"Not really," I smiled. "But it will be worth it, when the baby comes."

"Trish," she said, suddenly serious. "Have you thought about how you might feel if the baby's a girl? You know, with the way you worry? How would you cope with a daughter?"

Outwardly, I tried to shrug it off. But it was as though she'd dropped a heavy stone into the still waters of my soul and the ripples spread far and wide. Too far and too wide. Yes, what if? I was barely coping with Craig, or anyone else, being around my two sons. I could not begin to think how I would react to having a daughter.

"I'll just have to wait and see," I told her, with an unconvincing smile.

As if it was fate, my 20-week scan, at Tameside General Hospital, showed I was expecting a girl. It was lovely news, especially after two boys, but I felt a bizarrely bittersweet mix of excitement and dread. We were extremely lucky, but my instincts were right. This was a completely different dynamic. I felt like I was walking, blindfolded, into unmapped territory where at any time, I might fall headlong into a deadly crater. It must have been tough for Craig, wondering how I'd view him, how I'd trust him, with his own daughter. But he never showed it, and he was always so supportive to me.

In April 2019, our daughter Jessica was born, weighing 6lbs 3ozs and, like her brothers, she was the image of her daddy and was blessed with his beautiful big blue eyes. She was a miniature princess and from day one, we showered her with love and affection. I vowed she would have everything I had missed out on, in my own childhood. But those germs of uncertainty, which had threatened the framework of our family before, now suddenly multiplied and spread at an alarming rate. The very first time Craig changed Jessica's nappy, when she came home from hospital, I felt a chill run through me. I didn't like this one bit.

With difficulty, I bit back on my objections, but made sure

I kept a close eye on her. For what? I asked myself angrily. What are you watching out for? What kind of mother carried out covert checks on her own faultless husband? Craig was a wonderful, devoted, loving father. He was the best parent, the best husband, I could have wished for. So why on earth was I inspecting his every move, tracking him around the house like a sniffer dog? When bath time came, I stepped in, ready, with a new white towel over my arm.

"Honestly, let me do the bath," I insisted. "Please."

Craig nodded but I knew he was hurt. How could he not be? I was pushing him out, ostracising him, stifling his relationship with his own children. It was harmful for our children and for our marriage too, yet I just couldn't help myself.

"I'm sorry," I mumbled.

But I knew that didn't solve anything, and my anxieties hung over us like a guillotine, waiting to fall and chop our relationship into two. One afternoon, when Jessica was around three months old, Craig was changing her nappy. The two boys were watching with interest, keen to help by passing a clean nappy or a cotton wool ball. I was perched on the edge of the sofa on high alert, supervising closely, as always.

After he'd removed Jessica's nappy, Craig lifted her high into the air, and blew a raspberry onto her stomach. She giggled and the boys fell about laughing uproariously.

"Again! Again!" Jacob yelled.

But my insides were cold and hard as stone. I could not even force a smile.

"Give her to me please," I said, my words clipped and sharp. "I'll finish her nappy."

The boys stared, disappointed, as though I'd poured a jug of cold water over their fun.

"Are you OK?" Craig asked in a low voice.

Typically he was more concerned for me than he was for himself, but we both knew this could not carry on. Day to day, I was doing my best to quell my fears, but they rose up, hissing, like snakes, at the slightest provocation. I felt drained by the stress; weak and grey, as though all the colour had been leached from my life. Sometimes, my trauma was so actual and real, I could hear it whistling and screeching in my head. The sound reminded me of my guinea pigs; the kind of noise they probably made as they were sliced to death.

Craig's parents were always very keen to baby-sit and help out, especially after each new birth, but I would not hear of it. I could not bear the thought of leaving my babies with someone else. Craig often suggested arranging nights out, for our anniversary and birthdays, but he had to cancel them all.

"I can't leave the children," I told him. "I just can't. I'm sorry."

His mum lived nearby, and she was forever offering to pop over and look after the kids so I could get my shopping done or go to the hairdressers. But I could not allow it. I didn't take my eyes off them even for a minute. Running on a constant loop in my head was a long list of potential dangers which could affect my babies; paedophiles, murderers, car accidents, illnesses… If Jessica so much as snuffled, I was shot through with panic. I was constantly flipping between wanting a doctor's opinion, to then avoiding doctors because of my own experiences as a child. I remembered my father's obsession with exaggerating my own illnesses and I shuddered. I wanted no comparison with him.

Paradoxically, my over-protectiveness, my over-mothering, was affecting my ability to be a parent myself. Whilst I was so busy scrutinising everyone else's behaviour towards my children, I was not being the kind of mother I wanted to be. Physically, I was there, and I was a good parent, but emotionally, I was in turmoil.

By the spring of 2020, I felt I could take no more of it. All I had ever wanted was a family and a love of my own. I had it all now – and more besides. Yet I was destroying it and dismantling it, chunk by chunk, from within. What was wrong with me? Was it my fault? Had my father been right all along? It certainly seemed that way to me. Much as I loathed the parallels, I could not help comparing this self-destruction to his; he had dreaded prison, the threat had hung over him like an axe. And yet, he deserved to rot in there for the things he did.

On a different level, I dreaded losing my family. I did not know what I'd do if I ever lost Craig or my children. Yet I was driving them all away. Like my father, I was ploughing on with behaviour which I knew would lead to me to utter desolation and despair. I hated any link between me and my dad. I hated being like this. Deep down, I still did not believe I deserved to be happy. But I knew Craig and my three children deserved happiness and so I came to the biggest decision of my life.

* * * *

When Jessica was fifteen months old, in the summer of 2020, I made a call directly to the police.

"I'd like to report my father for child abuse," I said, with my hands shaking so much I could barely grip the phone.

"I've tried to report him several times before but now, I really feel I need to see this through."

The officer took some details and arranged for two specialist officers to visit me at home later that month. It was the fifth time I'd tried to make my voice heard and if I was honest, I had little hope of success, but I was desperate. I booked in with a therapist too. Craig was encouraging and kind as always, driving me to my appointment and waiting for me outside. I started seeing the therapist twice a week, and with his help, I slowly began to iron out my irrational distrust of anyone who came near my babies.

The two police officers who came to my house were professional, patient and understanding. I described to them, firstly, the sexual abuse in the bedroom and in the car.

"Always in the marital bed?" they asked, and the reference was jarring.

It was my parents' bed, of course. I had never let myself consider the relevance of this before. Was this another little kick for my father, yet another perversion, that he liked to abuse me in the bed he shared with my mother? I would never know. With my head spinning, I moved next onto the details of what happened in the living room.

"My father made me…. have sex…" I whispered.

The police officer cleared her throat.

"He raped you," she said. "Is that what you're saying, Trish?"

The word was like a sharp electric shock. I gripped the sides of the chair and stared at her.

"Rape?" I repeated, as though it was a foreign sound.

I had never seen it as such. Or never allowed myself to see it as such. For years, I had buried the abomination which had ripped me into pieces behind the stained-glass door, in the deepest recesses of my consciousness.

I could not, would not, allow myself to give it that name. But now it came to me in a blinding flash, in a sickening thud. I ran through every permutation, forcing myself to confront the monster which had been lurking in my mind for nearly 30 years. It was rape. I had been raped. My father was a rapist.

The realisation left me icy-cold.

"The next stage will be a video interview, at the police station," said the officer as the session came to an end. I saw them to the door in a daze. But long after they had left, the word screamed and flashed inside my head like a belisha beacon. It scraped away at the lining of my mind. It lodged in my brain like a parasite and it would not go away.

Rape.

When the day of the video interview came around, I woke to feel a rising panic in my chest. And during breakfast, I got a text from the police, reminding me to appoint a solicitor.

"A solicitor!" I gasped. "I had no idea I needed my own solicitor?"

"That doesn't seem right," Craig frowned. "Ask them about it when you get there."

He had offered to come with me, but he needed to look after the children at homeso I went alone. A female officer met me at the front desk, and, in an uneasy effort to make conversation, I said:

"I've never been in a police station in my life."

The officer looked straight through me, as if the last thing she needed in her busy morning was me making small talk.

"I'm sorry," I added. "I'm just really stressed about this."

"Oh," she harrumphed and showed me into a small room.

"Can I please ask about this, before we start?" I asked nervously, showing her the text about the solicitor.

"That's a mistake," she said dismissively. "Just ignore it."

And from there my panic dissipated into a sort of hurt resignation, an awareness that, even on attempt five, this was not going my way. Squirming in my chair, I answered as accurately as I could as she fired one question after another at me. She was digging over the wounds of my childhood, but her technique was so robotic, she may as well have been running through her shopping list. I felt sure she was briskly ticking off each question.

"And the sexual assault in the car? On the way to – from – the doctor?"

"And the timing of the assaults – always the same?"

"And the conversation - always the same?"

My hyper-vigilance was on high alert and I examined every barely perceptible movement of her facial muscles; every minute aspect of her body language. I got the distinct impression that she wasn't interested. I was an inconvenience, a burden. I was reminded of how I felt when I failed an assignment in high school. Even worse, I felt the officer didn't believe me and it was my job to convince her I was telling the truth. After I had brutally relived the early sexual abuse, the rape, the oral sexual assaults in the car, I reached the point where, when I was nine, my father was jailed for child sexual offences.

"What?" she exclaimed, perking up immediately. "I see. Right, well, let's go over your earlier story again."

It was another harsh twist of the knife. I was only being taken seriously because he had done it before. I wanted the officer to believe me, to focus on me and my trauma. I didn't want to piggyback onto someone else's ordeal. Was that too much to ask? The interview limped to a close and I couldn't wait to get out of the stuffy little room.

Back in the sanctuary of my car, I laid my head on the steering wheel and wept. I had spent years as a lonely child, a troubled teen, a mixed-up mother, waiting and hoping for someone to listen to me. I had tried to report the abuse five times. Now I'd finally made it to the police station. And still, nobody was listening. I felt like giving up; on justice and also on myself.

"How was it?" Craig asked when I got home.

I shook my head dully.

"I don't know," I replied. "I'm not sure it's worth it. I just feel like the police think it's not that much of a big deal."

Craig circled me in his arms and said:

"I think it's a big deal. You think it's a big deal. Don't give up. You know we're on your side, me and the kids."

Not for the first time, I was unpicked by his kindness, and I cried on his shoulder; tears of frustration at the system which had failed me, yes. But also tears of gratitude that I had a man like Craig in my corner. And I knew he was right. I owed it to myself, to my own children – and most of all to all the children my father might meet and target during the rest of his life – to continue pressing for justice.

That night, I had my recurring dream of running down corridors, hotel corridors, school corridors, underground corridors, pursued by so many men that bunched together, they looked like one solid mass. One big man, with one giant head. I ran and ran and ran. But I could not run fast enough.

I woke screaming and screeching, with a loud whistling in my ears, and another reminder of how my poor guinea pigs must have suffered. A couple of months later, I got a letter from the police informing me my case had been passed to the Cheshire force and I was required to give a second video interview at Macclesfield Police Station.

"Not again," I groaned. "I can't do it."

But then I received a call from an officer named Lee who told me he would be taking charge of my case. Even on the phone, my hyper-sensitivity was quickly allayed. He was professional yet understanding and patient.

"I'm sorry about the second interview," he told me. "But we need as much information as we can. It's important we get this right for you."

The second video interview was nothing like the first. It was tough, undoubtedly, going over it all again. But this time I really felt as if the officers were listening.

"All I want is accountability," I told them. "I want my voice heard. I want people to know what he did."

I came home and, for the first time in my life, there was a small glimmer of hope that justice might be possible after all.

27

The Road To
Justice

Early in 2021, I was in the kitchen peeling vegetables for a roast dinner when I got a call from Lee.

"I have some good news," he began. "The CPS have authorised charges against your father. Indecent assaults between 1993 and 1997, gross indecency, between 1993 and 1997, and a charge of rape, between 1993 and 1997.

"I'll be in touch soon, Trish. I just wanted to let you know, it's going ahead."

My thoughts were spinning in all directions, like an emotional waltzer ride.

"What does this mean?" I spluttered. "Is it going to trial? Will I have to go? Will I have to see him? What if he comes after me? What if he denies it? Will he go to prison if he's convicted? He hates prison. Remember, I told you that in my interview."

I was painfully aware I was babbling, lobbing questions at Lee like one of those automatic practice machines which spits out tennis balls.

"Trish, don't worry," Lee replied. "Let's take it one step at a time."

When I hung up, my breathing was fast and shallow. I couldn't believe it was happening. This was it. This was actually it. Since the age of six, I'd been waiting for someone to listen. And now that they were finally taking notice, I was terrified. Would I rather they didn't? Could I really see this through?

I didn't sleep at all that night. The adrenaline rushed through me in torrents. Each thought yanked me in a different direction; my father was a monster, he deserved to be punished. My father couldn't help it, he was just made this way. My father was terrified of prison, which was precisely where he deserved to be. My father had let me down. My father didn't know any better. It was like poking an ants' nest. The next day, I called Lee back, and asked:

"How did he take it? My dad, how did he react to the charges?"

"Well," he replied. "He wasn't happy."

In that moment I visualised the jaw clenching, the dark eyes sinking into the facial fissures, the eruption of a deadly temper.

"Oh, I said, in a small voice. "No, I can imagine. Thank you."

As I ended the call, I was flooded with fear. What if dad came after me, targeted me or the children? What if he was angry and decided to seek retribution? He had warned me, all those years ago, how much he hated prison. Now, if the case went my way, he'd be going back there. I couldn't begin to imagine how furious that would make him. He didn't know where I lived. He didn't even know my married name. But still…

"I'm so scared," I told Craig. "I feel like I've taken a huge risk."

My anxiety, always high, went into overdrive and I was deluged with possibilities and suspicions, each one increasingly unlikely and bizarre. I imagined him turning up in the middle of the night and plucking the children from their beds. I worried he might steal our family dogs. I had a dream where I was kidnapped and a large hand fixed me firmly in place on a giant chopping board whilst I was sliced up into neat sections just as my poor pets had been.

Each time my phone rang, every time there was a knock at the door, I panicked. After tucking the kids into bed, I spent hours looking out of Jessica's bedroom window, which overlooked the street, checking for strangers or strange cars. I made a note of our neighbours' car registration numbers so I'd easily recognise unknown vehicles.

During the night, if I couldn't sleep, I crept into Jessica's room and scanned the street outside for intruders. I spotted the odd fox, the occasional shift-worker. But that was all. My unease was made unbearable by the fact that I didn't know what my father looked like anymore. I hadn't seen him since I was nine years old. I wasn't sure I'd even recognise him if I bumped into him. The realisation was terrifying. I was looking out for someone, but I had no idea how to identify him. My father, for so long the bogeyman in my thoughts and dreams, now became a sort of faceless monster, an evil entity, without shape or detail but petrifying nonetheless.

Not long after, I heard my paternal aunt had died. I didn't attend the funeral but a relative texted me afterwards to say they had seen my father, who was now working as a lorry driver. The information was at once completely useless and absolutely crucial to me. Now, as well as checking the street for strangers, I began inspecting every single lorry I saw. As I was driving along, I'd crane my neck to peer into lorry cabs and assess the driver. Of course, I'd no idea who I was looking for, less still what I would do if I ever spotted a man I suspected might be my father.

In my mind, I fantasised about confronting him and watching him crumble, falling to his knees in remorse with the apologies tumbling from him like cathartic rocks in a landslide. It was a fantasy, I knew that. He would never take responsibility. It was not in his DNA to recognise his faults; easier always to pass the blame onto a child. Besides, I had been warned I was not allowed to approach my father because it might jeopardise the case. Even if I found him, I would have to ignore him. But I couldn't help myself. I checked every lorry I saw. It was a compulsion, an obsession which controlled me.

Thanks to therapy, my anxiety over my children's safety eased and though it could never be eradicated, I was at least able to leave them at school and nursery, and the controlled environment was a comfort to me. It also meant I was able to return to work as a teaching assistant. But near the primary school where I worked, there was a lorry park which served a local depot. I'd never taken too much notice of it before. But now it was simultaneously a rare gift and a fatal curse.

Each morning, after dropping the children off, I waited outside the lorry park so I could monitor every vehicle driving in and out. Again, I had no idea who I was looking for or what I would do. I was obsessed with tracking him down, and also terrified of doing so. Invariably, I was late for work, arriving with my clothes damp with sweat and the tell-tale red rash crawling up my face.

"Trish, are you OK?" asked one of my colleagues. "You look so flustered."

I managed to smile.

"I'm fine," I said. "Just a bit rushed, you know how it is."

I had been warned not to discuss the case with anyone at all. I couldn't tell any of my friends or colleagues about the police charges. And how could I tell a teaching colleague that I had been following random lorries in the hope, and dread, of seeing my paedophile father who had raped me as a child? No. Instead, I carried my secret around with me like a demon in my head, an evil jack in the box waiting to burst out. Midway through 2021, I got another call from the police.

"Your father has entered no plea in court," an officer explained. "The case will go to trial."

I was wrong-footed, baffled. I didn't even know it was possible to enter no plea. Deep down, I'd always expected my father to deny the charges. Nothing was ever his fault;

not a lost TV remote control, not a filthy kitchen, not an abused daughter. Why would this be any different? Yet this was the only thing I had ever asked of him. This was the final thing he could do for me. I just wanted him to be honest and again, he had failed me.

"The trial date is set for April 2022," she continued. "We'll be in touch nearer the time."

At first, I thought I'd misheard. I hung up the phone in disbelief.

"The trial is almost a year away," I told Craig. "I can't wait all that time. I can't live with this pressure. I just want to give it all up."

As always, Craig was the voice of reason in a mad world.

"Look, if you drop the charges, the stress won't disappear," he pointed out. "You still have to live with the trauma. And you will be so disappointed with yourself for not seeing this through. You've come this far. I know you can do it."

I resolved to put it to the back of my mind as best I could. My weekly counselling sessions continued to improve my concerns around the children. I started off by walking to the top of the street and back on my own. Then, I did the weekly shop, leaving Craig at home with the three children. I even had a drink with some of the school mums one evening. I still could not bear to leave them with anyone except Craig or his parents, or at nursery and school. But slowly, I was learning to trust.

"You're making brilliant progress," Craig beamed. "Well done."

In therapy, I finally confessed my horror and my grief at

the loss of my pets; my poor hamsters, rabbits and guinea pigs who were so cruelly slaughtered. And, worse still, the odd disappearance of Tyson and Bonnie. I had never found out what happened to them and the not knowing hurt so much more.

"It sounds as though you never had a chance to work through your loss," my therapist commented. "And it's not too late for you to do this. Let's think of a way for you to remember them, but remember them with love."

In the end, we decided I should paint a set of plant-pots in tribute to my pets. I had always loved art and I found it so cathartic, painting images of my cute little rabbits and hamsters onto every pot. A fat tear rolled down my cheek as I painted a picture of Tyson's big brown eyes and his one white paw.

"Miss you, Ty," I whispered. "Always will."

After the paint was dry, I planted yellow roses in each pot and each day, watching them flourish and bloom, I had a feeling of well-being and cleansing, as if my sadness had turned full-circle. I realised my animals being so thought-lessly forgotten and dismissed had hurt nearly as much as their deaths.

It was the same issue when I was reporting the abuse; I wanted recognition, I wanted to be heard. Being trampled upon and ignored was not OK for my pets and it was not OK for me. Now, with their faces looking back at me from each plant pot, and the roses thriving above them, I felt the memory of my pets had been suitably honoured at last.

* * * *

In the New Year of 2022, with my trial date drawing nearer, I was called back to the police station to recap my interviews and statements. It was now becoming frighteningly real. During one meeting, a female officer handed me a set of forms and said:

"Trish, you should consider applying to the Criminal Injuries Compensation Authority."

I took a moment to process the words and then I said furiously:

"I don't want money! I'm not doing it for money! My husband and I both work hard. We don't need it, thank you."

It wasn't like me to lose my temper at all, less still to raise my voice, and I immediately began to apologise.

"Just think about it," she urged. "You've lost a lot, financially, because of the abuse. This is a chance to get a small amount back."

Still, I felt deeply offended, but I thanked her, and the moment Craig came home from work, I offloaded my frustrations.

"Can you believe it?" I fumed.

"I think it's a good idea," he said calmly. "You spend a lot of money on counselling. You've spent a lot of time with the police. Think of all the years you went from job to job, struggling to get by because your mental health was a mess. Think of how much easier your life would have been without the abuse."

It was an impossible dream. And yet, without the abuse,

perhaps I wouldn't have found myself on a dating site and I would never have met Craig. I reminded myself that I had achieved happiness in spite of my abusive past, not because of it. I was not at all comfortable with the concept of compensation, but I made the application because I trusted Craig's advice. I received £23,000 in 2022 which would go on to cover the costs of my ongoing counselling.

As part of the prosecution case, the police had applied for both my social services and medical records. I was given copies and one night, with the children in bed, I braced myself to read the hefty file which was several hundred of pages thick.

One paediatrician had written:

'The current problem seems to be one of having some good days and having other days when she feels generally tired and washed out…the most important thing is trying to ensure that she gets to school.'

Other doctors again expressed concerns I was missing a lot of school and suffering night-time seizures and one letter linked my mother starting a new job with long working hours to my poor health.

"My health deteriorated because I was left in the house on my own with my father," I said sadly. "It was nothing to do with my mother's job. The jigsaw pieces slot together perfectly when you have the full picture in front of you."

In just a few months, I had missed 71 days off school, with 'generally off' and 'generally awful' symptoms. Another letter said I 'hadn't been back to school this term' at all.

The notes confirmed that I never had fits at school or,

with three exceptions, during the day. They were all at night when nobody else except my father was aware of them. A doctor had even written to my teacher to ask about my health. My teacher replied to say the school was not aware of any seizures or any other health issues. Their only concern was that I was never there! I found many examples of my father exaggerating, even fabricating my symptoms too. One doctor said:

'As before, our impression is that there may be slight over-reporting of symptoms and it is not entirely clear whether Patricia's problem in the last fortnight is due to her seizures or not...'

There were countless examples of my father bringing forward appointments or requesting extra help because I had suddenly deteriorated.

The notes said:

'... the possibility that Patricia's continued attacks are mis-interpreted as seizures.'

And again:

'It has been noticed she has tended to wet the bed... and seems disoriented first thing in the morning. Father was wondering as to whether this represents evidence of nocturnal fitting which clearly it might. I therefore suggested putting her dose back up again...'

Another record said of my symptoms:

'I am not convinced they have any organic origin to them at all... she has been extensively investigated previously and we have not found any abnormalities that would indicate a more serious underlying organic condition... I have explained I don't think there is a lot we can do from a medical point of view...'

Another doctor said: '... sounds typical of breath-holding attacks and not fits.'

And another: 'I'm just a bit concerned... she doesn't seem ill enough...'

During one of these appointments, my parents claimed I had lost 1kg in weight, to which the doctor responded:

'I must admit I am a little suspicious...as she doesn't look as if she has lost any weight...'

And there was much more:

'... brought a whole load of other concerns forward... I tried to play down various complaints as Patricia looked very well...'

'I must say I am not sure that all of the events reported... are convulsions.'

'Perhaps a tendency to accentuate symptom reporting.'

'Is she really having nocturnal fits?'

'... there is no actual definite evidence of epilepsy in this record as there was in the previous one..'

It was as though my father was hell-bent on me being ill. There were references to the infamous 'Family Fund' and also to my family's application for Disability Living Allowance (DLA) on my behalf. One letter, written by one of my doctors, read:

'I would be reluctant to write in support of the application for the family fund on behalf of Patricia King. I don't feel that she comes close to the criteria you outline... she is so far outside your normal criteria that I would suggest you don't pursue the application very far. Certainly Patricia had problems in the past which might possibly have put her into the criteria and there is considerable parental anxiety over Patricia's continuing health, but as a result of treatments and growing older, Patricia is becoming stronger and healthier… this does put me in a difficult position with Mr and Mrs King…'

Was my illness a cash cow, a gift horse, an unexpected but hugely beneficial side effect of the sexual abuse? It was win, win, win for my father. He had tried to control the doctors, pulled their strings like puppets, just like he had controlled me. I was angry, bitter, appalled. But most of all, I felt sad. Sad and sorry for the little girl who was caught up in this awful mess. I read on and came across the notes relating to the time the nurse had washed my hair in the bath. I remembered the scent of the bubble bath, the luxury of the occasion, and it made me smile, even now. The nostalgia was so powerful.

In other records:

'It was noted family hygiene was unsatisfactory'

'In the past the house was of poor hygiene and that this might be contributing to Patricia's problems.'

There followed a year or so where I missed appointments and one letter reported the family phone was disconnected. There were numerous letters chasing up missed appointments. Most likely those letters lay in our hallway, stacked up alongside the unopened electricity bill and the council tax.

"Best place for them," I muttered.

I was about to go to bed, I had been reading for ages, and

my eyes were closing. Craig had already gone up earlier. But then, flicking through some of the later pages, a passage from a social services report caught my eye – and my heart stopped.

'… reported that there were concerns that Patricia may well have been abused. Over the past year she has been wetting the bed and she has had soreness down below which had been put down to the drugs she was receiving for her epilepsy. It may be that she will begin talking at some time in the future.'

My vision seemed to blur. I wasn't sure I had understood it correctly. I had to read it again and again. I ran upstairs, woke Craig, and asked him to read it also.

"Bloody hell," he said, the colour draining from his cheeks. "They suspected all along. They suspected you were abused."

For what felt like an age, there was a heavy and oppressive silence weighing on my shoulders. And then, it burst from me like a haemorrhage.

"She will begin talking at some time in the future!" I gasped. "I spent years telling them I'd been abused. I wrote it down. I verbalised it. I put it in a letter, in an essay, in a phone call. I told a counsellor, a teacher, and a social worker!

"How could they? How could they leave me like this?"

I worked out the report had been written after my father was jailed, when I was around 9 years old. In the years that followed, I had done all I could to report the abuse, save pasting it on a giant poster or screaming it on national TV. I remembered the desperate letter I had written to social services when I was 14.

The realisation they had suspected all along was like a scalpel slicing through my soul. I thought of my poor pets and their gruesome deaths and I felt something of their pain. The fact that a social worker had suspected I might have been abused and had done nothing did not make me angry. It broke me inside. It made me feel dull and defeated and totally alone. Why had nobody helped me?

28

The Trial

By the time April 2022 came around, Jacob was five years old, Oscar was four and Jessica just two. Though I had never left them with any extended family members or friends, they had a close relationship with their paternal grandparents.

"Why don't we ever see your daddy?" Jacob asked me one day. "Where is he?"

I hesitated. I had pernicious feelings of guilt that the children didn't know my father. No matter how much Craig insisted it wasn't my fault, I felt responsible all the same.

"Why can't I see him?" Jacob asked again.

At first, I was tempted to tell him a white lie; brush off his curiosity by announcing my father was dead or living abroad. It was the easiest option, but I knew it wasn't the right one. In years to come he could easily find out the truth online and I owed it to him to be honest.

"My daddy did bad things and he hurt me," I told Jacob.

"That's why we don't see him."

There was a moment while he digested the information. And then, Jacob's soft little hands balled into fists and his eyes shone with a fierce loyalty.

"I am mad with him," he told me, in the angriest voice he could muster. "I will hurt him back for you mummy, don't you worry."

"Oh Jacob," I said, biting back tears. "Come here and let me cuddle you. You don't have to fight anyone. A cuddle is always better than a fight. Don't you forget that."

Craig was called to give evidence at the trial, as well as myself, and we were faced with the unavoidable prospect of leaving the children overnight for the first time. Because we were required at Chester Crown Court early in the morning – and it was more than an hour's drive from our home – the police had suggested we stay in Chester.

Craig's dad, Steve, and step-mum, Julie, had offered to look after the children at their home in the West Midlands. It was a kind gesture. I knew I was lucky to have such accommodating in-laws. But the idea of my children spending the night away from me was even more stressful than the worry of me appearing at the trial and giving evidence.

"How are they going to manage away from us?" I fretted.

What I really meant, and I knew it, was how was I going to manage away from my children. I knew Craig's family were more than capable of looking after the children. Oscar had been unwell with mumps and chickenpox which made me feel even more concerned about leaving him. But both he and Jacob were giddy with excitement when they discovered they were going away on their first ever sleepover. Jessica was too young to understand but she was swept away with the general atmosphere of delight.

The day before the trial began, we packed their overnight bags; pyjamas, teddies, Disney-themed toothbrushes. I was so frantic and the guinea pig whistling in my head was so loud, I could barely concentrate. I kept on packing and repacking the same items. We drove down the M6 that afternoon and seeing the children so animated and excited when they saw their grandparents really put my mind at rest.

"Please, don't worry," Steve assured me. "We'll take good care of them."

I knew that. I felt awful that he had to say it. But as we drove away, and the court case loomed like a spectre at the end of our journey, I was seized with anxiety again. Was I doing the right thing? Craig and I had booked into a hotel in Chester; our first night alone away since Jacob was born. Yet it was hardly a romantic break. We went out for dinner and I couldn't swallow a single mouthful. I felt as though I had an epilepsy tablet jammed in my throat. It was like being a child all over again. It was all streaming back; it was all too much.

"Let's go back to the hotel," Craig said. "Don't worry. You're going to be OK, Trish."

At the hotel, I checked and rechecked my outfit, convinced I had forgotten one of my shoes or my skirt. I had chosen a black pencil skirt, black shoes and a high neck pink jumper. The high neck was picked out specifically to hide the mottled rash which I knew would cover my chest and neck during cross-examination. I didn't want the judge or the jury to see me so anxious and uncomfortable. But more than that, I didn't want my father's barrister to see the rash because he would know the occasion was getting to me. I was determined not to give him that satisfaction. To wear underneath my jumper, Craig had bought me a silver dinosaur, on a chain, with the children's initials JOJ written inside a heart. Oscar was obsessed with dinosaurs and had insisted Craig chose a dino pendant. It was the most beautiful piece of jewellery I had ever seen.

"When it gets tough in court, you remember your necklace and you'll be fine," Craig told me.

I barely slept the night before the trial. In fragments of broken dreams, I spotted a man who looked just like my father from the back; he was wearing one of his usual Polo shirts, with a crumpled collar. As he turned, I braced myself, and then froze in terror. For though he was human from the neck down, he was faceless, and there was a blank, empty space where his features had once been.

I woke, pinned to the bed with fear, shrieking out in panic. hen I finally managed to calm myself and fall back to sleep, I had the same broken dream again, it went round and round on a loop. But each time, the faceless spectre which spun around to confront me, was as blank and as terrifying as ever. The following morning, exhausted but wired with adrenaline, I was up early and ready. Even as I pulled on my pink jumper, I could feel a giveaway rash sneaking across my chest. I had been promised a screen in court, so I didn't need to see my father at all. Perhaps, I thought, he might remain faceless to me for the rest of my life.

"Ready?" Craig smiled.

He looked so handsome in his suit and his polished shoes, and despite everything, I felt a swell of pride and love.

"You scrub up pretty well," I beamed.

"You're not so bad yourself, Mrs Hinde," he laughed and took my hand.

But on the walk to the courthouse, my unease grew and grew. We arrived far too early, and Craig suggested we grab a coffee and sit by the river to pass some time. It seemed like a good idea, sitting in the spring sunshine, watching a mother duck and her ducklings waddling along the riverbank.

"Look," I said to Craig, pointing out the line of ducklings. "How lovely."

But as I spoke, a large seagull swooped and snatched the smallest ducking from the back of the line. I cried out as I watched its tiny, webbed feet flapping as it was swallowed alive. I could not help thinking of my hamsters, my rabbits, my guinea pigs. I could not help but think of my six-year-old self. The whistling began again in my head, louder, shriller, more piercing than it had ever been before.

* * * *

Still rattled by the death of the poor duckling, we approached the main doors of Chester Courthouse. I glanced at a man in a dark jacket who was smoking a cigarette outside, right by the door. Suddenly, there was a whooshing noise around me, smashing so loudly against my eardrums I couldn't hear anything else. I felt my legs wobbling and giving way and Craig's arm reached out to steady me.

"Trish!" he exclaimed. "Trish? What's the matter?"

The ground zoomed up, almost smacking me in the face. A nuclear explosion could not have derailed me more violently.

"It's him," I gasped, suddenly short of breath. My lungs felt flat and airless as though they'd been popped.

"Oh my god, it's him. Craig, it's him."

The moustache had gone. The face was older. The body was a little thinner, more angular maybe. He wore a smart, dark, jacket; I couldn't remember ever seeing him in a jacket. But the eyes; those sunken black eyes were exactly the same. *The eyes.* It was the eyes which gave him away. The craggy contours of his face were so aggressively defined that they seemed like separate components rather than parts of this odious man as a whole.

"Don't look at him," Craig whispered. "Don't speak to him."

With our heads down, and Craig's arm tight around me, we stumbled past him. He was with a woman, presumably his partner or his wife. Once inside the foyer, I dashed to the ladies to splash my face with cold water. Well, I had a face now for the faceless bogeyman.

The irony was, I thought I didn't know what he looked like, I presumed I wouldn't recognise him in the street. Yet I would have known him anywhere. I could have picked those dead eyes out of a crowd of millions. Those eyes had seen me at my lowest. Those hands had stolen my childhood. That man was evil. How could I have dreamed for a moment I might forget his face? After I had cooled my cheeks, I reapplied my make-up and checked myself in the mirror. In a flash, behind me, I saw him again. He was headless this time, disembodied, hanging just under the fluorescent lights. I shuddered. The eyes looked so sunken and so sad.

"What did he think when he saw me?" I wondered. "Was he proud of me?"

It was a sucker-punch. Even now, as I was about to face him in court for abusing and betraying me in the evillest way imaginable, I wanted my father to be proud of me. It wasn't a thought I wanted to have. But I couldn't help it. That conflict, that confusion was still there. He was a monster. Yet he was my dad.

We had an early meeting arranged with the prosecution barrister, who was very apologetic; clearly something had gone wrong in administration for me to be greeted by my rapist at the court doors. He also told us any kind of exchange or altercation with my father could well have jeopardised the case.

"We didn't even look at him," Craig assured him. "We were aware of the risks."

The barrister went on to explain something about levels of sentencing in relation to the sexual assaults my father had committed against me. But his words washed over me. I was fixated by headless images of the craggy, worn-out skin and the sinking eyes.

"My questioning may seem brutal and extreme," the barrister warned, but I barely heard him.

In court, I was shown to the witness box. The judge and

jury were already in place and, as I searched the faces of the jury, I suddenly spotted kind and gentle eyes, which reminded me so much of the ghost lady. I half expected the jury member to be wearing a long Victorian dress with ruffled sleeves. The compassion radiated from her, just as it had from my ghost. In that moment, I felt a calm and peace rolling over me. The Ghost Lady was here. I was going to be alright. I felt for my dino-necklace, hidden under my pink jumper. Yes, I was going to be fine. I was hidden behind a screen before my father was brought into court. It allowed me to see the jury, the judge and the barristers. But not him. Then, the prosecution barrister stood up.

"Can I ask if your father licked your vagina more than twenty times?" he asked.

The court was silent, but the horror, the revulsion, was palpable, passing from person to person, like a deadly electric current crackling around the room. I sank back into my chair and wished it would swallow me. I was mortified.

"Yes," I said quietly.

Secondly, I was asked to confirm that the letter, written by me to social services about the sexual abuse, was indeed my writing and my work.

"Yes," I said again.

And that was it. The prosecution barrister had finished with me. Still reeling from the first question, I tried to prepare myself for the defence barrister. I thought again of the ghost lady, sitting in the jury in human form, I thought of my dino necklace and they soothed me. I felt strong. I felt courageous.

Naively, I had assumed each barrister would be given equal time to cross-examine me. Instead, after just two questions from the prosecution, I now faced over 90 minutes of an aggressive barrage of accusations, demands and insinuations from my father's defence team.

"So, what colour was the family car when you were six years old?"

"And where were your siblings when the abuse was apparently happening?"

He stressed the word 'apparently' which rankled with me, but I thought of the ghost lady on the jury, I felt the cold metal of my necklace against the heat of the rash and I kept my focus.

"And did it happen in half-term, or term-time?"

"And did he ever make you undress fully?'

It went on, and on and on.

"I don't know," I replied truthfully. "I don't know. I was a small child. I can't remember all the details. But I do remember being sexually abused and raped."

The barrister changed tack and moved on to the letter I had written.

"How old were you when you wrote the letter?" he asked.

"About 11," I replied.

"Well, I have news for you," he said smugly. "I can categorically prove you were aged 14 when that letter was written."

Despite myself, I felt a surge of irritation.

"I don't see what difference that makes at all," I snapped. "I was 14, so what? That period of my life is a blur because of the trauma, because of the passage of time. 11 or 14, I was still a child. I was an abused child, crying out for help. Picking at my age or my memory doesn't change that."

There was a beat of silence. Then the barrister asked me:

"Have you seen your father recently? Have you been in touch?"

I shivered.

"I didn't see him for many years, but yes, I saw him this morning, on my way into court. He was standing outside, smoking, when I arrived."

There was a rustle around the court and the judge told the prosecution barrister in no uncertain terms to keep my father right away from me for the duration of the court case. The hearing was adjourned for a short break and though it was a relief to be able to gather my thoughts, I wasn't allowed to see Craig because he was a witness too.

After a quick cup of weak tea from a vending machine, it was time to go back into court and be pulled apart once again. I was being hollowed out, bit by bit. The defence barrister accused me of bringing a case against an innocent man for financial gain in reference to my application to CICA. His comment was so far off the mark, it was laughable.

"I'm not interested in money," I retorted. "I'm not even too concerned about the conviction or the sentence. All I've ever wanted is for the truth to come out."

When the cross-examination was over, I felt drained, but also strangely composed and calm. In a funny way, I felt I'd had my moment. I had done it. My voice was heard. My job was done. On my way out of court, a lady from the CPS smiled at me and mouthed:

"Well done," and just those two words really lifted my spirits. I felt positive, regardless of the outcome of the trial. Craig was not, in the end, called for questioning and so we were free to go home. I was told the trial would last a further five days and the officer, Lee, had promised to call me when the verdict was in.

"You did really well in the witness box," he told me.

I could only hope it would be enough.

29

A Bittersweet Verdict

Back at home, there was no time for me to dwell on the trial. Ozzy was still recovering from mumps and chickenpox and was only just ready to return to school. Jessica's birthday was coming up too, so I was busy planning her party, buying and wrapping gifts.

For a few days, I managed to push it all to the back of my mind. But on the fifth day, I could not concentrate at all. Craig had booked the day off work and after taking the children to school and nursery, I went back home, planning to catch up on my ironing, clean the windows, maybe pay some bills. But my head was whistling and screeching.

"Let's go for pizza," Craig said at lunch. "Pass some time."

I was looking at the menu in the restaurant, sipping a lemonade, when my phone rang.

"Tell me!" I begged, the moment I answered. "Please just tell me!"

He was found guilty of nine out of eleven charges," Lee told me. "Well done, Trish. You did it. I'm proud of you and you should be proud of yourself. He's been remanded for sentence tomorrow."

I couldn't even formulate a reply.

"Thank you," was all I could manage.

I hung up and stared at Craig who was scanning my face for signs of joy or devastation. But I felt numb. Completely numb. There was no celebration, no party. There was no winner here. I had done it. But it had nearly finished me.

The following day, Lee called again to say my father had been sentenced to 15 years in jail. I felt a rush of jumbled and paradoxical emotions. It was a long sentence, yet no sentence could ever be enough. How could he ever be suitably punished for trying to destroy me? I had thrived and found happiness, despite having him as a father. His abuse could easily have killed me too. If he died in prison, it wouldn't be long enough.

For me, the case had never been about a conviction or a sentence. It was all about someone listening to me. It was all about being believed. Him going to prison was an additional bonus. Yet I couldn't help worrying about him too. He hated prison, he was scared of it, and I had put him there. I had purposely condemned him to the place he was most terrified of, possibly for the rest of his life. In that moment, I was six years old again and I felt so small, so afraid.

"You did the right thing," Craig told me. "This is all part of his manipulation, passing the guilt onto you, making you feel bad for speaking out about what he did. He brainwashed you. It was his way of keeping you quiet for so long."

Even so, when I saw my father's mugshot online later that night, I felt a pang of undeserved compassion. His eyes looked so sad, so defeated. The report read that Gerard King, 59, of Bury, Greater Manchester, had been found guilty of one count of rape, five counts of indecent assault and two counts of indecency with a child under 14. The court heard he had put me through: 'truly horrifying systematic abuse'. He was jailed for 15 years plus one year on extended licence.

Following the sentencing, Detective Constable Lee Ferris, who led the investigation, said: "Firstly, I would like to recognise the bravery and determination that the victim has shown throughout this investigation.

"She had previously reported the offences, on several occasions, to numerous professional agencies, but had never built up the courage or received the support she needed to take the case further.

"When she came forward to police in 2020 we provided her with the specialist help and support she needed to ensure that she was able to tell her story.

"What King put her through was truly horrifying, he systematically abused her over a three-year period in order to fulfil his own sexual gratification.

"Not only that, but he also made her endure a trial and recount what he had done, which was extremely distressing.

"But thanks to her courage, he is now facing the consequences of his actions.

"The sentence handed to King reflects the severity of his crime and I hope that his conviction will encourage other victims to come forward.

As this case demonstrates, we treat all reports of historic sexual offences seriously and we will always do our best to ensure offenders are brought to justice."

I looked again at the mugshot. It was the only photo I had of my father. Not the sort of keepsake a daughter would normally treasure of her father.

"Would he be proud of me and my family?" I wondered again. "Would he?"

I was angry with myself for wanting his approval. Yet as Craig said, this was all part of the grooming process. Child abuse by a family member is never black and white. There is no true justice for victims because deep down, there is a tiny germ of doubt, of guilt, of shame which lives on. No amount of counselling, no lengthy sentence, no public support, could erase that. So, though I knew my father deserved to be in jail, I could not celebrate it.

The days after my father was jailed were surreal. And gradually, as the reality sunk in, I felt, if not celebration, a definite feeling of relief and pride. I was satisfied that other children were now safe from my father. I was pleased that in years to come, I would be able to tell my own children that I had stood up for truth and for justice; that ultimately my voice was heard.

It was important, as their mother, that I showed them that silence is never the answer to abuse. It was a lasting regret, but not a surprise, that he had shown no remorse whatsoever. At the trial, he had the opportunity to admit his guilt, he had the chance to say sorry. And he chose not to take it. I had hoped for an apology, yes. But I had never expected it.

So many people from my childhood got in touch, many saying they had suspected him for years. A couple of former teachers and friends contacted me, confirming they had been worried about me as a child. Their delayed sympathy left a bittersweet taste. If they had suspected I was in danger, why was nothing done to help me? Ryan, my first boyfriend, who I'd hadn't heard from for over a decade, messaged to say:

'Glad someone finally listened and believed you to take it further, brilliant news.'

I was genuinely glad of his support, and his words triggered a flashback in time. I was 14 again, hanging around the skatepark, skipping school, overdosing on lip balm and body spray. They were times of deep and appalling trauma, but oddly, I looked back on them fondly. Now though, I realised I had survived despite my father, despite the dreadful circumstances, despite being failed time and time again. Despite reporting my abuse five times and four times being ignored. I survived thanks to Tyson, thanks to the Ghost Lady, thanks to Baby Expressions. I survived also, thanks to myself.

At aged 35, I could finally begin to give myself some credit. Only now, I saw my father's abuse for what it was; toxic, evil and warped – and totally and completely his fault. And after years of not talking about my childhood through shame, misplaced loyalty, legal constraint, or – despite five attempts – because nobody would listen, I suddenly wanted to tell everyone. I wanted to shout it out and most of all to reach the children who, like me, keep secrets. Because secrets are never a good thing and I would like this to be the lasting message from my story.

Afterword

In 2023, thanks to the wonderful support network around me, I have found true happiness. I am currently working as a complaints manager and Craig is a financial crime operations manager. Despite the success of my therapy sessions, the legacy of the abuse lingers and it always will. It manifests tangibly; I can't bring myself to drink cream soda or dandelion and burdock and I loathe dark chocolate. My father used all these as bribes and softeners and I can't get past that.

I struggle to swallow tablets too. I took so many as a child, most of them completely unnecessary and I get that tell-tale lump in my throat, like a jammed pebble, every time I take so much as a paracetamol.

In bed, I cannot have Craig's arm around me. Occasionally, in his sleep, he might unconsciously fling out an arm, and I am snapped suddenly awake; hot with panic. I cannot bear to be trapped or hemmed in. I cannot bear to be cuddled. It is a tragic consequence of my father's abuse that he took something so innocent as a loving embrace and poisoned it.

I remind myself every day he is in prison, I know I am safe, but still my hypervigilance gets the better of me sometimes. If I hear a car door slam or a raised voice outside, I automatically run to the windows to check the street.

When I take the children out, I am always on the lookout for danger, for potential threats. Again, as with those months before the trial when I checked every lorry I saw, I don't really know what I'm looking for. But it's a compulsion, and the trick I've realised is just learning to live with it. Still, I don't leave the children with anyone outside the family. I am preparing myself to bend these rules as the kids get older with sleepovers, school trips and sports tours. I've loved giving my children roots. It will be so much harder for me to give them wings too, but I'll do it.

Physically, I have recovered remarkably well from a childhood dominated by fake and genuine illness. I have recently been diagnosed with Irlen Syndrome, which is a problem with the brain's ability to process visual information. I have a sensitivity to light which means I have to wear tinted glasses, even indoors. After growing up in a household where nobody saw what was really happening, where nobody dared look either side of their own limited tunnel, it is ironic that I now have issues with my vision. And yet in many ways, I see more clearly now than I ever have.

Our children, Jacob, Oscar and Jessica, now aged six, five and four, bring us so much joy. Jacob is the double of his daddy and loves science and superheroes; he is caring and loving and is always ready for a cuddle. He has his own funny little posh accent and speaks very well. He is going to be our academic. Ozzy loves to hide behind doors and jump out, adores play fighting and football and is obsessed with dinosaurs. He is going to be our action man. Jessica really loves creepy-crawlies, especially worms, and can often be found chasing her brothers with bugs in her hands. I feel as though I've come full circle;

after my own childhood was plagued with nits, Jessica now actively seeks them out! She has many little idiosyncrasies; she likes odd food combos, like dipping chips in strawberry milkshakes or blackcurrant juice. They are choices which make the rest of us squirm. She is going to be our comedian.

I will never forget the love and warmth my pets brought me when I was a child and I want that for my own children. They have two sausage dogs, Amber and Astra, our old Labrador, Autumn, a bearded dragon, a gecko and four gerbils.

Family life is fabulous. I look back on the past and it was undeniably horrific. But then I consider my present, and my future, and it is undeniably wonderful. I feel proud I have broken the cycle of abuse and misery and that my own children are growing up in a loving and stable home. To top it all off, we added to our brood on 12 December 2023, with the arrival of our beautiful daughter, Ohana. She was born after just two contractions, with Craig racing to the hospital and arriving just in time for the birth. We all adore her and she has made our family complete.

As for my father - a title he does not deserve - I never want to see him ever again. The one man who should have loved and protected me instead tried to destroy me, and at times, he very nearly succeeded. I asked one thing only of him, to admit his guilt in court, and he would not even do that for me. I no longer feel guilty that he is in jail because I've finally realised it is precisely where he belongs. And if being in prison scares him and upsets him, then he has only himself to blame. I have learned, after 30 years of holding myself responsible, that none of this − none of this at all − is my fault.

Acknowledgements

I would like to acknowledge my therapist Andrew who has saved my life. Also my mother-in-law Sue who has been there throughout and has supported me without judgement from day one of meeting her son. You are the shining example of a mother's love.

Other bestselling Mirror Books written by Ann Cusack

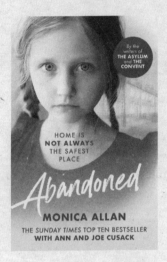

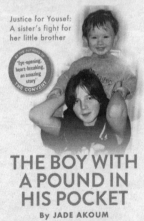